# The Postmodern University?

*SRHE and Open University Press Imprint*
*General Editor*: Heather Eggins

# The Postmodern University?

Contested Visions of Higher Education in Society

Edited by
Anthony Smith and
Frank Webster

Society for Research into Higher Education
& Open University Press

Published by SRHE and
Open University Press
Celtic Court
22 Ballmoor
Buckingham
MK18 1XW

and 1900 Frost Road, Suite 101
Bristol, PA 19007, USA

First published 1997

A catalogue record of this book is available from the British Library

ISBN 0 335 19958 5 (pb)   0 335 19959 3 (hb)

*Library of Congress Cataloging-in-Publication Data*

The postmodern university? : contested visions of higher education in
   society / edited by Anthony Smith and Frank Webster.
         p.   cm.
      Originated from a colloquium held at Magdalen College, Oxford and
   Oxford Brookes University, July 19–21, 1996.
      Includes bibliographical references and index.
      ISBN 0–335–19959–3 (hb). — ISBN 0–335–19958–5 (pb)
      1. Education, Higher—Social aspects—Great Britain—Congresses.
   2. Education, Higher—Social aspects—United States—Congresses.
   3. Educational change—Great Britain—Congresses.   4. Educational
   change—United States—Congresses.   5. Postmodernism and education—
   Great Britain—Congresses.   6. Postmodernism and education—United
   States—Congresses.   I. Smith, Anthony, 1938–  .   II. Webster,
   Frank.
   LC191.8.G7P67   1997
   378′.01—dc21                                                97–16128
                                                                   CIP


Typeset by Graphicraft Typesetters Limited, Hong Kong
Printed in Great Britain by St Edmundsbury Press Ltd., Bury St Edmunds,
Suffolk

# Contents

# Notes on Contributors

*Zygmunt Bauman* is Emeritus Professor of Sociology, University of Leeds. He has been Chair of General Sociology, University of Warsaw, 1964–8; Professor of Sociology, University of Tel-Aviv, 1968–71; and Professor of Sociology at the University of Leeds, 1971–91. Professor Bauman's many publications include: *Legislators and Interpreters* (1987), *Modernity and the Holocaust* (1989), *Intimations of Postmodernity* (1991), *Thinking Sociologically* (1991), *Postmodern Ethics* (1993) and *Life in Fragments* (1995).

*Phillip Brown* is Reader in Sociology at the University of Kent at Canterbury. He has written, co-authored and co-edited a number of books, including *Schooling Ordinary Kids* (1987) and *Higher Education and Corporate Realities* (1994, with Richard Scase). He is currently completing an anthology on education, economy, culture and society with A.H. Halsey and others, and writing a book on capitalism, class and social progress in the twenty-first century (with Hugh Lauder).

*Paul Filmer* was educated at the University of Nottingham and the London School of Economics. He is Co-ordinator of Taught Postgraduate Studies in Sociology and of the interdisciplinary programme in Contemporary Cultural Processes at Goldsmiths College, University of London. He has taught at City College and the Graduate Center of the City University of New York (1970–2), and has been Visiting Professor at the University of California, San Diego (1974 and 1987–9), Guest Fellow in Social Sciences at Columbia University, New York (1971–2), and Visiting Fellow in Comparative Literature at Monash University, Melbourne (1989). He has been consultant to the Arts Council of Great Britain's Research Committee (1976–80), to the Crafts Council (1980–3), and to the Laban Centre for Movement and Dance, London, since 1978, where he is also a member of the Centre's management committee. He has served on a number of editorial boards and has recently been a specialist subject assessor in Sociology for the Higher Education Funding Council. His main publications include *New Directions in Sociological Theory* (1972), *Language Theorising Difference* (1974) and *Working in Crafts* (1983).

*Russell Jacoby* is presently Adjunct Professor of History, University of California at Los Angeles. He was born in New York, and educated at the Universities of Chicago, Wisconsin, and Rochester. His fields of interest include twentieth-century European and American intellectual and cultural history and history of education. His main publications include: *Social Amnesia* (1975), *Dialectic of Defeat: Contours of Western Marxism* (1981), *The Repression of Psychoanalysis: Otto Fenichel and the Political Freudians* (1983), *The Last Intellectuals: American Culture in the Age of Academe* (1987), *Dogmatic Wisdom: How the Culture Wars Divert Education and Distract America* (1994), and an edited collection, *The Bell Curve Debate: History, Documents, Opinions* (1995).

*Krishan Kumar* was educated at St John's College, Cambridge and the London School of Economics. He has been Professor of Social and Political Thought at the University of Kent at Canterbury. He is currently Professor of Sociology at the University of Virginia, where he moved in 1996. He has been a BBC talks producer, a Visiting Scholar at Harvard University, a Visiting Professor at the University of Colorado at Boulder, and a Visiting Professor at the Central European University, Prague. His main publications include: *Prophecy and Progress* (1978), *Utopia and Anti-Utopia in Modern Times* (1987), *The Rise of Modern Society* (1988), *Utopianism* (1991) and *From Post-Industrial to Post-Modern Society* (1995).

*William Melody* is Guest Professor and Chair, International Advisory Board, Centre for Tele-Information, Technical University of Denmark, Lyngby. An economist by training, he has spent his career working at the interface between academic research and teaching, and public policy development and implementation. He was founding Director of the Centre for International Research on Communication and Information Technologies (CIRCIT), Melbourne, 1989–94; and the Programme on Information and Communication Technologies (PICT), Economic and Social Research Council, UK, 1985–8. Melody was Senior Research Associate, St Antony's College, Oxford, 1987–9, and a Professor at Simon Fraser University, British Columbia, 1976–85, and the University of Pennsylvania, 1971–6. He has published widely on the communications industries, technologies, economics and public policies. He has authored articles on communications and information technology issues in the *Canadian Encyclopedia* and the *International Encyclopedia of Communications*. He has undertaken policy research studies and consultancies with local, state, national and international organizations.

*Richard Scase* is Professor of Sociology at the University of Kent at Canterbury. He has authored, co-authored and edited 15 books, including (with R. Goffee), *Reluctant Managers* (1989), *Class* (1992), and (with Phil Brown) *Higher Education and Corporate Realities* (1994).

*Peter Scott* was educated at Merton College, Oxford and the University of California at Berkeley (Graduate School of Public Policy). He is currently Professor of Education and Director of the Centre for Policy Studies in Education at the University of Leeds. From January 1998 he will be Vice-

Chancellor of Kingston University. From 1976 until 1992 he was editor of *The Times Higher Education Supplement*, and was previously a leader writer on *The Times*. He is Vice-Chair of the Lord Chancellor's Advisory Committee on Legal Education and Conduct and a member of the board of the Further Education Development Agency. He published *The Crisis of the University* in 1984 and his latest book is *The Meanings of Mass Higher Education* (1995).

*Anthony Smith* has been President of Magdalen College, Oxford since 1988. He graduated from Brasenose College, was a BBC current affairs producer between 1960 and 1971, a Fellow of St Antony's College from 1971 to 1976, and Director of the British Film Institute 1979–88. He has served on the Board of Channel Four Television, and has been a member of the Arts Council and the Acton Trust. His many publications include: *The Shadow in the Cave: The Broadcaster, the Audience and the State* (1973), *British Broadcasting* (1974), *The Politics of Information* (1978), *Goodbye Gutenberg – the Newspaper Revolution of the 1980s* (1980), *The Geopolitics of Information* (1980), *From Books to Bytes* (1993), *The Oxford Illustrated History of Television* (1995) and *Software for the Self: Culture and Technology* (1996).

*Frank Webster* has been Professor of Sociology at Oxford Brookes University since 1990. He was educated at Durham University and the London School of Economics. He has also taught at Ealing Technical College (1974–8) and the University of California at San Diego (1981–2). He has served as Hon. General Secretary of the British Sociological Association (1993–5), chaired the Heads of Sociology in Advanced Further Education (1989–92), and was a member of the 1992 Research Assessment Exercise panel for sociology. His publications include: *The New Photography: Responsibility in Visual Communication* (1980), *Information Technology: A Luddite Analysis* (1986, with Kevin Robins), *The Technical Fix: Computers, Industry and Education* (1989, with Kevin Robins), *Teaching Sociology Handbook* (joint editor, 1993), and *Theories of the Information Society* (1995).

# Preface

This book springs from a colloquium jointly organized by the editors, Anthony Smith and Frank Webster, and held at their respective institutions, Magdalen College, Oxford and Oxford Brookes University, over the weekend of 19–21 July 1996. Funding for this co-operative venture, between an ancient college established more than five hundred years ago and a university created as recently as 1992, was supplied by the Fulbright Commission, to which we extend our hearty thanks. The Commission was prepared to sponsor the colloquium without pre-conditions, an invaluable and rare act in these times.

The aim of the colloquium was to consider the character of the university in a period of radical and rapid change. To this end were assembled a number of interesting and able intellectuals, all with extensive experience and knowledge of university life, in the UK and abroad.

It is truistic nowadays to say that university education and experiences are undergoing major change. Mass higher education is rapidly becoming the norm, changed means of funding it are being developed, and new means of accessing and analysing information and knowledge are becoming widely available. Being a student or an academic at university in the 1990s is significantly different from a generation ago. Simultaneously traditional purposes of the university are challenged, and with this also conceptions of the student and of the academic vocation. Arguably the Anglo-Saxon model of the university (élitist, residential, cloistered) is giving way to a more North American and European model which is more open and connected to the wider society. There is a considerable professional literature on how best to manage these changes – how to teach effectively to larger classes, how to be more 'entrepreneurial' – and there is a good deal of public concern about matters such as maintenance of standards and how best to resource our universities and our students.

What has been lacking in the UK to date is sustained intellectual reflection on these changes. In the USA there are a number of key texts – from the work of Martin Trow to that of Allan Bloom – as well as an established

body of research literature on higher education, which helps to conceptualize and understand what is happening in the university, and with what
consequence. We set out to support the development of such a literature.
Accordingly, this book reflects the concerns and contributions of intellectuals from inside and outside academe whose first priority is not to manage
the changes, but to conceptualize and better understand them.

Somewhat to the editors' surprise, the weekend discussions quickly divided
between, on the one hand, those who adopted, with more or less enthusiasm, the vocabulary of postmodernism to account for changes in higher
education, and, on the other, those of a more recognizably modernist turn
of mind. The former welcomed a perceived plurality and differentiation of
the postmodern university – its flexibility, its refusal of authoritative expertise
and legitimate knowledge, its capacity to shift and change. The latter, where
they saw signs of a postmodern condition, tended to be critical, though
most were unconvinced that changes had been so profound as to justify any
'post' labels.

This debate provided a ready structure for this book. Part 1 pits proponents of the postmodern university (Bauman and Scott) against the un-
persuaded (Kumar and Filmer). In our introductory chapter we try to give
a flavour of the context of the discussions and their substance. Part 2 takes
the debate on to universities in the public sphere, providing for the most
part, it must be said, a counter to postmodern interpretation with a spirited
attack on intellectual life inside today's universities (Jacoby), a call for
universities to act in the public interest (Melody), and a forceful reminder
of social inequalities in higher education (Brown and Scase). Our final
chapter presents a review and assessment of the debates.

We thank our participants for making the weekend so exciting, engaging
and challenging. They were: Zygmunt Bauman (Leeds), Laurence Brockliss
(Magdalen College, Oxford), Phil Brown (Kent), David Caute (independ-
ent author), Paul Filmer (Goldsmiths College), Alan Howarth (MP, Strat-
ford), Michael Ignatieff (independent author), Russell Jacoby (University
of California at Los Angeles), Krishan Kumar (Kent, now University of
Virginia), David Marquand (Sheffield, now Mansfield College, Oxford), Bill
Melody (Technical University of Denmark), Geoff Mulgan (Demos), Melanie
Phillips (The *Observer*), Ben Pimlott (Birkbeck College), Peter Scott (Leeds),
Jean Seaton (Westminster), Theodore Zeldin (St Antony's College, Oxford).

In the preparation of the book much helpful advice and support came
from Lisa Lucas (Warwick), Tim Blackman (Oxford Brookes) and Alan
Jenkins (Oxford Brookes), each of whom provided valuable guidance on
relevant literature.

# 1

# Changing Ideas of the University

*Anthony Smith and Frank Webster*

## Introduction: the university as imagined community

The university has tended to absorb and accumulate the changing aspirations – and perhaps also the presumptions – of successive generations and, not surprisingly, it has also come to disappoint them. The community of scholars was once seen as a model of rational and disinterested discourse and thus has come to be regularly pilloried for the proclivity of academics to factionalism and internecine dispute. The politicized desire for a 'multiculturalist' resolution to ethnic conflict has forced the same community of scholars into accepting a range of ritual policies affecting curricula, appointments, symbolic self-presentation, as if the university possessed the tools of direct and easy social leverage. Today, the university is also expected to treat its students as consumers, and so students have begun to blame their teachers for their failures; there is even a new trend for failing students to sue. In the course of the expansion of university places in the 1960s a complex bureaucratization took place which contributed to this new mix of expectations a rational management of knowledge through the organized augmentation of scholarship and research; the nation-state fused cultural and scientific knowledge into a mutual metaphor and the university has been expected to succeed in such paradoxical goals as fostering, through 'culture', the creation of a sort of democratized managerial élite while training a mass of scientists to underpin the industrial requirements of a nation operating in a competitive global economy. It is hardly surprising that the terms 'training', 'education', 'scholarship' and 'excellence' are buried like unexploded bombs beneath all discussion of the future of universities.

Nowhere in western Europe have the changes in the nature of the university as institution accelerated so rapidly as in Britain, where the pace and profundity of reform have perhaps been exaggerated because of its relative lateness in making the move from élite to mass higher education. The most obvious symptom of change in British higher education has been the dramatic increase in student numbers: there are presently 1 million full-time students in the UK, a number which has leapt from 600,000 during the 1990s alone. In the early 1960s the number was a fifth of the present total. Today one in three young people go to university, a proportion which is continuing to rise. Where it was once thought exceptional to win a place at university, was a guaranteed sign of academic and social advance and a just occasion for celebration, today it merely marks a stage in life, requiring no special academic merit, signalling in itself no great likelihood of later worldly success.

The expansion has been accompanied by a squeezing of resources, as is now widely acknowledged, and this has manifested itself in growing student poverty, declining academic salaries, falling academic social status, and in the increasingly shabby fabric of universities themselves. With the growth in student numbers has come a devaluation in the currency of a degree, with graduates no longer feeling confident of achieving high salaries and high status in later life. And alongside this decline have come the charges that standards are declining and that universities are awarding (in the words of *The Sunday Times* of 3 September 1995) 'dummy degrees'.

The dramatic expansion has been made possible as a result of the arrival of a host of new institutions bearing the title 'university'. In Britain, a vision of the traditions of an ancient institution immediately springs to mind at the very use of the term 'university,' but the truth is that very few of them are old: fully three-quarters have been founded since the 1960s and, most dramatically, 30 of them were dubbed universities overnight in 1992. Along with these transformations has arrived the novelty of university 'management'. Once upon a time the head of a university would be an academic, chosen as the *primus inter pares* of a *collegium* of scholars. Today, the typical managerial figure in a university is the chief executive/vice chancellor, on a six-figure salary, brandishing a strategic plan and without high-level academic achievements of his (still much less frequently her) own.

These are not, of course, the only visible signs of change. Perhaps the most far-reaching has been the impact of the revolution in information technology which has naturally swept through the campuses of the world as epicentres of information-generating activity. The universities have been foremost among institutions proclaiming the information revolution and pioneering the use of the computer and new forms of communications as alternative tools for learning and research. The new technology has also suggested itself as a means of spreading teaching beyond the physical and geographic confines of the campus as traditionally conceived.

But these changes are propelling a fresh round in an ancient and continuing debate about the role of the university, about what Cardinal Newman (1987), writing in 1853, highlighted as the *Idea of a University*. For much of this century the 'Idea' of the university has been, or has appeared to be, a straightforward, if not settled, matter. It was unashamedly an élite institution which was attended by at most a twentieth of the population. Dons were upper middle-class people who mostly seemed to belong to the cloistered atmosphere of the campus. Their job was to expose students to what Matthew Arnold had in 1867 described as 'the best that has been thought and known in the world' (Arnold, 1983, p. 31). The primary purpose of the university was 'the pursuit of true judgment' and within the realm of knowledge there existed a clear hierarchy of themes and skills. When a graduate emerged from the process he (usually) evinced characteristics which distinguished the 'educated' person from the 'uneducated'. There was much local diversity but the ideal, the motivating force, was universal and seemed obvious for most of the century from 1860 onwards.

Of course, universities were very different in 1960 than in 1860, perhaps more than any other reason because of the relentless trend towards subject specialization as society and economy demanded greater and greater expertise. There was a steady process of differentiation and splintering of zones of knowledge which rendered it increasingly hard to state the goals which were held in common by all areas of the academic community (Clark, 1983, p. 18). Writing at the turn of the century, Max Weber (1948, p. 243) observed that the separation of the expert from 'the cultivated man' underlay the then prevailing debates about the purposes of higher education.

The dilemmas produced waves of stress and anxiety within the academic community. For instance, Sir Walter Moberly (1949, p. 50) could write about the 'chaotic university' which was sensing the strain between the call to instruct and the call to investigate, the demand for democratic admission procedures and the gradual movement towards more 'applied' roles. None the less, if the post-war era brought an end to the unitary idea of the university, it still seems that plural ideas could be made to cohere (Kerr, 1963), the university welding together its teaching and research roles, as well as its concerns for the well-being of students and the unconstrained pursuit of knowledge as an active ideal.

That account hardly amounts any longer to the prevailing Idea of a university, at least as applying to Britain's hundred-plus university institutions. It would not resonate today, say, in the University of Sheffield, still less in the Universities of North London, Luton or De Montfort – and even less does it seem to illuminate university curricula leading to degrees in business administration, accountancy and retail management. The problem of description goes deeper than a mere finding of the right words. It has become evident that the modern university has changed in purpose, perhaps beyond recognition in many cases. Today's universities are so diverse, so fractured and differentiated that it may have become absurd to seek to express any grand organizing principle. John Newman's 'Idea' never really prevailed, anyway. A vast section of the population was excluded from the possibility of sharing in the benefits of the university institution. But it probably was the case that for a time a single discourse about the university did resonate at least throughout the academic community and the educated public of the time. What has become clear in current discussion about the function of the university is the absence of any attempt to give expression to a general motivating theme.

One striking characteristic of British higher education in the present era is its seeming passivity, despite the energy which universities today invest in political lobbying and in public relations. The offices of vice-chancellors and managers of corporate communications are clogged with press statements and fliers proclaiming the achievements of their students in obtaining employment, how effective their institutions are in inculcating 'enterprise skills' into their graduates, how successful in their co-operation with industry, how energetic in their contribution to the wealth-creating resources of the nation. Where one speaks of passivity, no suggestion is being made of a lack of energy or initiative. But there is a marked reluctance to articulate a motivating purpose, to address questions about the *raison d'être* of higher education. The discourse we do have is a relatively unedifying and certainly uninspiring one – it is the constantly reiterated defence of the university in terms of its usefulness to government and industry (Readings, 1996). The university seems resigned to a pre-set agenda which is narrowly instrumental, one can say passive.

There are some voices within the university who find themselves genuinely galvanized by this agenda and loud in their enthusiasm for such projects as 'breaking down the ivory towers' and placing the university in the 'real world'. More common is the reluctant resignation to what is happening, the mumbled coffee-time rejection, or the passing sneer at the latest course in 'entrepreneurial achievement'. But no alternative vision seems to be available, and the main explanation which arises readily in every mind is, of course, the demoralization widely felt after almost two decades of economic exigency and government stricture.

This circumstance is manifested in such phenomena as stalled careers, job insecurity and the repeated intervention of officialdom (including ministers) in academic matters. Academic life has become much less attractive than in the past (Halsey, 1992). In the heady post-Robbins era of the 1960s resources flowed, jobs abounded and the university seemed to be an institution of society with a burgeoning future, consulted and respected by government. Today the condition of the academic profession is dominated by fear of redundancy, an atmosphere of penny-pinching, with jobs shrivelling into short-term contacts. The most deafening sound is that of educational consultants advising the profession how 'to teach more cheaply' (cf. Scott, 1984).

Many institutions have lost the sense of intimacy with their students – the dialogistic experience declined when it became increasingly difficult to teach through seminars with half a dozen participants, scarcely possible in today's groups of 15 and more; in their place has come 'distance learning', 'self-guided instruction', the mass lecture, and workbooks intended to substitute for live dialogue between teacher and student. Then there is the urgent pressure to generate income in order to sustain the employment of one's colleagues and oneself which has given rise to a sense of the inevitability of a generalized professional compromise: money-making consultancies have become a goal, the booking of profitable conferences and the identification and pursuit of research projects the purpose of which is to win resources rather than enhance knowledge. The mentality of the modern university has become survivalist, dominated by a sense of the duty to endure rather than enjoy. Articles are published to satisfy the judges of the Higher Education Council; additional students are taken on to one's stint or module – but all with a heavy heart and a weariness that undermines the educational mission and belies the academic ethic.

These are prominent topics in almost every contemporary discussion of the university's problems. But there are wider contextual contributing factors: the historian David Caute emphasizes various dimensions of the *Zeitgeist* in the post-communist era, of the vitalization of the 'end of history' theme. The collapse of the Eastern European regimes, barbarous as they were in the eyes of practically all Western academe, has fostered a wider disillusion with all publicly owned and funded institutions. Any public organization, whatever social benefit it aims to provide, is for the moment tarred with the brush of intervention in the free market environment (cf. Anderson, 1992). There is a quiet suspicion that all such institutions are somehow doomed, or at least doomed not to be successful. The credo of Mrs Thatcher has been reinforced since the events of 1989, in the way in which voices critical of the workings of free markets in any sphere have tended to fall silent.

Another of these wider factors bearing down upon the new conceptualization of the university is the emergence of a widespread sense of the postmodern which tends to subvert many of the traditional justifications of the university. Zygmunt Bauman (Chapter 2) underlines this throughout his contribution. Postmodern thinking suggests that the academic community is a kind of fiction, and that *difference* is the hallmark within and between institutions which bear the title. The growth of specialization has become so complete that colleagues even within a faculty often cannot discuss their areas of expertise without misunderstanding. Standards vary within departments, still more across universities and between eras, and so it has become impossible to defend any particular hierarchy of subjects in the modern university today, let alone any notion of authoritative knowledge.

The environment is one of mutual contestation of knowledges. The circumstances of this 'multi-vocalism' inhibit the mounting of a defence of the university as the repository of this range of forms and versions of knowledge: there are many new open and accessible alternative sources of authority over knowledge – television, the Internet – and wherever claims to knowledge are made they are challenged. When difference is so strong a factor, fragmentation is the corollary. The confidence of intellectuals in their own activities has been reduced and there is no one available to speak for the university.

But it is still possible to urge that the university remains the primary site of cultural engagement and exploration. This is emphasized by Krishan Kumar (Chapter 3) who concedes much of the 'postmodern' case. Even where knowledge is uncertain and contested there exists the potential for a worthwhile intellectual endeavour, and this demands a physical location where people can come together and work together. Professor Kumar agrees that the university cannot be defended if it relies for its justification exclusively on the transmission of knowledge and skills since these are both challengeable and obtainable elsewhere. But his is one of the voices arguing for the survival of the university as we know it.

There is a view – expressed here by Russell Jacoby (Chapter 6) – that the growth of the university system has brought about a decline in the number of intellectuals who write for a wider public. This is in a sense another explanation of the passivity of the university community today. The traditional alternative sources of support for freelance intellectual activity (the little magazine, the patron-publisher) have declined and at the same time intellectuals have entered the university system *en masse* where they have become excessively professionalized, writing for one another, often in an abstruse style which might facilitate peer esteem but shuts out the non-specialist reader. The so-called poststructuralist school of thought provides the classic instance. One question hanging over the discussion is therefore whether expertise in a given subdiscipline or intellectual school necessarily confuses the intellectuals in communicating with the broader public.

Russell Jacoby shows how this can lead to absurdities such as self-proclaimed radicals, securely tenured at renowned universities, who insist that they are 'outsiders' in the world of prestige and privilege, while their writing is incomprehensible to the general public and has no impact other than to inflate their academic standing among similar people (cf. Said, 1994). On these terms, today's tenured professors, even if they wanted to articulate a purpose for the university today, would be incomprehensible to the people to whom they wished to deliver the message. But as it is, their concern for their own specialist enclaves, whether the rubric be post-colonialism, cultural studies or even marginality studies, is so intense that a general case for the university is difficult for them to think through.

Bill Melody (Chapter 7) reaches a similar destination but after taking a different route, one which reflects his long involvement as a policy-making economist. He discerns a 'welfarist' mentality in the university of today, an outlook of 'whinging and whining', which is ultimately both dependent upon and subservient to the public purse. As a consequence it has no voice of its own and, while it grieves about reductions in funding and bemoans the heavy hand of government, it takes what it can without questioning the basis of this disposal of resources. Professor Melody will have no truck with those who yearn for the time when higher education was left alone by politicians and industrialists, and when professors were free to research and to teach whatever they wished. He points out that university development has always been integrally connected with public policy – apart perhaps from an untypical élite among institutions which have amassed great wealth. The great expansion of universities took place to meet the employment requirements of an industrializing society and to respond to the research and development needs of that society. There is simply no future in imagining that the university might cut itself adrift from public policy since it has always been intimately linked. The real questions are only what the character of that public policy will be and how it will be established.

To Professor Melody it is astonishing, as we enter the information age in which a premium is placed upon timely and appropriate research, on access to knowledge, on ever more highly educated workers, that suddenly the university finds itself with so little to offer. The university seemed to be the *central* institution of the long proclaimed 'age of information' (Bell, 1976, p. 116 *passim*), in which it was to be the key location of intelligence, innovation and training. Yet today the universities are remarkably silent about their own contribution to this vast social transformation and they stand accused of a hangdog attitude, looking for scraps from government. This is particularly worrying, continues Melody, because it leaves the un-folding 'information society' to take shape along market principles without anyone stressing the consideration of wider public interests. While universit-ies themselves are being decisively influenced by these policies, there has yet been little debate about non-commercial or extra-commercial concerns such as the public right to information and the consequences of the commodif-ication of information. Few now in the university investigate matters that do not appeal, in some way, to the private corporation (Buchbinder, 1993).

So Professor Melody pleads for universities to be braver than they have been, to fill the vacuum in public policy by being more adventurous and by taking a lead. It might be that his advocacy is greeted by postmodern think-ers as unacceptably arrogant on behalf of academe, but is it not the case that the public interest is being left undefended?

## Making the case?

At the colloquium in which this book has its roots it was Alan Howarth, a former minister for higher education, who urged that universities recognize their powers, which remain considerable even in cash-strapped days. For a start, universities are essential to present-day society and are concomitantly the objects of aspiration on the part of an increasing proportion of the population. Moreover, they contain articulate and highly intelligent people who should be able to present persuasive arguments in their own cause. In the wider society, he claims, universities maintain a high standing and are the objects of admiration: it is hard to think of any influential centre of ideas which is not closely linked to a university. One has to look back to the very early years of the twentieth century, to the Bloomsbury circle, to recall a moment when an influential group existed substantially outside the university realm – and Bloomsbury, too, drew into itself a number of lead-ing university figures, from Maynard Keynes to Bertrand Russell.

None the less, universities ought not to look to politicians for their pro-tection. The Treasury is necessarily philistine in its operations, concerned to minimize public expenditure and thus unwilling to listen to grand ideas.

Politics is today pursued as a career, and ambitious politicians cannot be relied upon for support. Nor can the vice-chancellors be turned to for a positive defence for their record is one suggesting a lack of vision, responding as they have done opportunistically rather than defiantly or imaginatively to the sequence of problems which they have had to confront. Analysis of the widely touted 'mission statements', for instance, demonstrates a constant recourse to cliché, immediate self-interest and superficiality, almost all of them being describable as marketing statements (Watson, 1996). Their aim is only to ensure that they are as well placed as possible to deal with an immediate negotiation with government.

But a broad and profound case is available which does not side-step economic exigency, depending as it does completely upon a willingness to project the university on a grander scale than heretofore and beyond the merely instrumental. And the case has to come from intellectuals and academics themselves.

The university has become a crucial *rite de passage* in the development of citizens. It provides a transformative experience in people's lives when identities may be decisively shaped and lasting friendships and associations contracted (Pascarella and Terenzini, 1991). This is apparent to those who have the good fortune to pass through universities. Moreover, that university experience provides a basis for the cultivation of independence of thought which underpins a healthy democracy (cf. Barnett, 1994). This entails the provision of tools and realms of knowledge which provoke thinking (Anderson, 1993) which will better equip students to examine and evaluate the situations they will encounter later in life. The experience, moreover, enables the development of 'narratives of engagement' with present and past circumstances, an essential element of a vibrant culture.

Very close to this idea is the call for a reassertion of the principle of 'disinterestedness' which Paul Filmer (Chapter 5) discusses; this, too, underpins the modern university, hard though it is to identify this quality. It necessitates a commitment to the ancient 'academic dogma' of positive neutrality (Nisbet, 1996) which provokes the investigation of phenomena whithersoever the search may lead. The 'dogma' encourages a suspicion of all attempts to direct the university from without, though without being naïvely autonomist or over-confident. But the university experience does nurture a reflective quality and it is universal in those who have shared in the experience.

The university exerts an impact, a clarifying of the mind, and though it has become dangerous (and provocative when postmodernists are at hand) to identify this with a 'civilizing' mission, it should never be allowed to go unsaid. That is not to slip into a facile defence of the Arnoldian creed. George Steiner has placed so indelibly in our memories the fact that the Third Reich coexisted with the appreciation of Goethe and Mozart that no one can pretend that the university, or any other institution, is in itself an adequate protection against the forms which barbarism takes. And yet one is still left with the belief that higher education is surely a necessary ingredient of civilized society.

One participant at our colloquium who was uncomfortable with talk which might give the impression of a yearning for an era when the university was confined to an exclusive minority was Theodore Zeldin. He urged that universities should make plain that they are concerned with the 'arts of living', the means by which people explore the seeking of joy, the training of the emotions and the passions, ways of deepening experience. The university's role in the transmission of up-to-date knowledge is no longer an exclusive one and in the era of advanced communication technologies there are plenty of other ways readily available in which people learn 'how' to do things; but there is a powerful case opening up for universities to concentrate upon the entire life course and to act as a resource for facilitating personal and social development, the exploration of ways of living. For Zeldin one useful metaphor for the university was as a 'house of pleasure' into which one might pass at various times to recharge one's batteries, to enhance one's sensitivity, to improve one's life. A significant but marginalized and under-proclaimed dimension of university life is, of course, already concerned with this and, given that the post-employment era of life is expanding in Western societies, the university might concentrate upon this growing and largely unacknowledged function. It should be promoted as an integral part of the role of the university in modern life.

In his review of the postmodern world and the university's place within it, Peter Scott (Chapter 4) stresses the increasing disconnections between education, work, lifestyle and identity which once were or appeared to be parts of a self-consistent pattern. But education today no longer leads to a specific source of employment with a guaranteed style of life associated with it. The 'identity' of an individual is no longer a subset of work and lifestyle. But the university could emerge as the key institution in offering people the opportunities they need to develop their potential beyond the directly economic and to find ways to associate with others with whom they feel common bonds – to build and mould their self-image. The university can thus offer a sequence of opportunities of retraining at each era of life.

## Credentials and jobs

Is it necessary to accept that there is no longer an Idea or perhaps a group of ideas which unifies the university today? Are we henceforth to resign ourselves to the descriptions of the university as a 'conglomeration' with 'multifarious missions' and 'numerous disparate elements' (Clark, 1983, p. 26)? Zygmunt Bauman (Chapter 2) and Peter Scott (Chapter 4) are both convinced that the postmodern university is characterized by diversity, disagreement and difference – from top to bottom. In this case there can no longer be any call for an 'Idea' of the university and, indeed, in Professor Bauman's thinking, we should be pleased with our 'good luck' in possessing this diversity and cease our search for an underpinning rationale. What gives our universities their defining purpose is that these institutions, however differentiated, retain the monopoly of the granting of credentials (now only a near-monopoly). Daniel Bell (1966) started saying this a long time ago when he drew upon the terms of sociology to depict the vast American university as having shifted from the world of 'community' – where there existed a strong sense of unity among staff and students – to the world of 'association' between diverse strangers between whom moral ties are minimal, from academic *Gemeinschaft* to academic *Gesellschaft*. In this scheme of things the humanities have nothing in common with the natural sciences, apart from the fact that all of the students seek credentials from the same institution as a testament to their achievement. The university has become an accrediting institution.

This train of thought is fraught with dangers: first, that the university may become reduced to a servant of the professions, employers and industry, and succumb to the penetration of the university by sponsors, by professional bodies seeking accreditation on their own terms, not to speak of the opportunistic search by some university departments for programmes 'of use to industry' which suggests that this trend is already well entrenched; and second, that the university risks being taken over by outside agencies if it defends itself only in these instrumental terms, since there may be others better equipped for the provision of skills. Geoff Mulgan of the *Demos* 'think-tank' felt this to be the case, and the astonishing growth of the 'corporate classroom' suggests that this could be pre-ordained. Perhaps we should heed Sir Douglas Hague's (1991) frequently expressed strictures on the university 'dinosaur' and his championing of the private enterprise 'knowledge entrepreneur' – we would see into a future in which business will make vast inroads into 'what one might have expected to be the university's province' (Hague, 1996, p. 12).

Of course there must be a link between success in higher education and achievement within the world of work, even if the connection arises simply through the extra motivation provided by possession of a university degree – and that in turn arising from the historic association between possession of a degree and access to a comfortable livelihood (Bonney, 1996). It is equally clear, however, that a degree no longer guarantees a good job; the phenomenon of the unemployed graduate has been apparent for long enough now for the sober realization to be widespread that present-day graduates are and will be underemployed in comparison with earlier cohorts. But the routes to high earnings and satisfying jobs are more firmly blocked to those who do not possess higher education.

This altering relationship between university and employment is the subject of the contribution of Phil Brown and Dick Scase (Chapter 8) who draw upon empirical work which they have recently undertaken into employment preferences within the changing business environment. There is a noticeable shift here from the bureaucratic career (where an employee works his or her way up through a hierarchy while demonstrating 'technical and conforming competencies'), towards 'charismatic employment' (where employees are expected to be team players, leaders, critical self-starters and so forth). As a result recruiters want graduates with the appropriate 'personality package', quite different from the 'organization man' of yesteryear, and more in keeping with the fast-paced and flexible needs of today.

At a time of overproduction of graduates this favours selection from the most prestigious universities, where students are presumed to have the appropriate transferable skills in their personality profile. (Where these skills are explicitly taught in the new universities, this is believed to be a consequence of the admission of inadequate students who require compensatory education!). The Brown–Scase team is deeply sceptical of the ambitions of many new universities which wish to prove their value by equipping their students with transferable skills. They think that selection is highly subjective, recruiters favouring people like themselves, rather than those possessing genuinely transferable skills. Students, especially the less privileged who gravitate towards the new universities, have yet fully to acknowledge this altered scene, and forlornly yearn for bureaucratic careers which are more amenable to planning, more openly fair (with clear rules and procedures) and less subject to the whims of patrons and sponsors.

This form of recruitment hinges on the 'positional location' of the university; that means, the higher the standing (social as well as academic) of the university, the more appealing its graduates are to employers and the higher are the 'transferable skills' which the students are presumed to have acquired. One key policy implication is that universities might be better advised to pay less attention to teaching transferable skills, seeking instead to improve their perceived position in the university ratings. These positions may appear to be set firm at the upper levels (where Oxbridge dominates), but there is certainly movement lower in the ranks (as witness Warwick's rise over the past 25 years, and the promotion of several of the new universities into mid-table positions).

## The university and social justice

If it is the case that recruitment of graduates favours those who attend the more prestigious and established institutions, then it follows that universities must have retained some 'old-style' features even in a post-Fordist economy where a premium is placed upon flexibility. This hardly proves the existence of a postmodern era in which, allegedly, differentiation leads to impenetrable complexity. The distinguishing traits seem to have remained clear, at least to potential employers. And so the patterns of recruitment also raise – and in acute form – the issue of what one might call social justice and the university.

Our colloquium listened to evidence of continued and even heightened social exclusivity in terms of access when it comes to the most highly rated universities. This has something to do with the changing distribution of occupations in society and, naturally, one might expect fewer students to come from homes where the breadwinner is a manual worker in a society in which manual work has greatly declined. But the situation appears to be worsening. Increasingly, the top tier of universities is being filled by the children of the professional middle class, those most able to supply the cultural (and often the material) capital that assists success in the extremely competitive entrance procedures (cf. Walden, 1996).

There is a paradox here. We are seeing an increased accessibility in higher education, but in parallel with this is a heightened competition for places at the top universities, a situation in which the most privileged are winning most of the awards and continue to seize the rewards when it comes to getting jobs. We are seeing the coexistence of greater inclusion alongside greater exclusion. This phenomenon is being exacerbated by the decline of the residential university largely because of its prohibitive cost to students. We may recall that Professor Kumar (Chapter 3) yearns for this, but the fact is that in 1995 almost half of all university applications were from candidates in their home region. Moreover, social inequalities are reflected in this shift. The Universities and Colleges Admissions Service reported recently that younger and better-off students still tend to live away from college, 'but rising numbers of older students and applicants from ethnic minorities are helping increase the stay-at-home trend' (*The Guardian*, 9 August 1996). Bluntly, the better-off still send their children, overwhelmingly at the age of 18 or 19, to a residential university, to acquire that which employers clearly most desire. It is mature students, those from disadvantaged homes, and ethnic minorities, who disproportionately represent those who live at home while they study at the local university. In turn, they lose out when employers come to make their choices about recruitment. There are no easy solutions to this injustice, but injustice it remains.

## The end of the residential university?

The residential university does have great appeal in this country, both to students and to academics, but Laurence Brockliss suggested at our colloquium that we might learn something here from our European neighbours. The Anglo-Saxon model of the university is markedly different from the French or German, where typically students study in their large-scale and local institution; the British ideal of 'intimacy' between teachers and students does not come much into play. If we mean to establish a system of mass higher education which is affordable, then the British university might cease to foster the expectation that it is a place of residence. It is well known that British universities are considerably more expensive to run than their counterparts abroad, so this might be a means of moving forward. Moreover, continued Brockliss, residency might have been defensible a generation and more ago, but today's 18-year-olds are so much more mature than their predecessors that a good deal of the broad educational case for it has gone.

One should also remember that the new technologies may now begin to be an increasing factor in the decreasing demand for residential education.

The frequently evoked scenario of the 'virtual university', in which students learn from and interact with leading academics irrespective of distance, is now, in principle at least, a practical possibility, even a reality (Laurillard, 1993). This technological solution to spiralling costs in higher education will have an inevitable appeal – perhaps excessively – to policy-makers.

But against this it can be objected that students as well as teachers required personal contact in the process of education – a computer terminal is an unsatisfactory alternative to students and to tutors. The evidence from the Open University – the great pioneer of distance learning – is that students have enormous enthusiasm for human interaction, summer and weekend residential schools being commonly regarded as the high points of their periods of study. Equally, and everywhere, we are warned against the easy assumption that technology can supply a substitute for 'live' teaching by tutors. Technologies are more often supplements than substitutes: television has not replaced the book, nor word-processors paper. Of course, computerized forms of instruction will develop rapidly in the next few decades, but the utopian policy-motivated predictions need to be treated with great caution.

Laurence Brockliss also questioned the British emphasis on the necessity and sustainability of combining teaching and research. Why should academics be expected to do both and be proficient at both? It is a clear matter of record that our most esteemed universities did not conduct research until the recent past; the phenomenon is relatively new, going back at most a few decades. It is salutary to be reminded that Newman's highly influential *Idea of a University* (1987, first published 1853) emphatically dismisses research from the university, leaving the latter free to give full attention to the students. Although many university teachers today clearly identify with and aspire to combining research with teaching, there is little evidence (Ontario Council on University Affairs, 1994) that undergraduate students benefit from or are even aware of the research conducted by their teachers. Indeed, the best evidence from the United States (where higher education is itself a subject of serious research) suggests a negative correlation between the research orientation of faculty and student satisfaction with the teaching that is provided, Alexander Astin (1993, p. 418) going so far as to conclude that 'the university's increasing difficulties in offering a high-quality undergraduate education can be traced primarily to the massive expansion of university-based research' which leads to the appointment, promotion and emulation of 'stars' who do not teach much, whose identies are defined through their research rather than through teaching, and who tend to eschew more student-centred and innovative forms of teaching (cf. Sykes, 1988).

There are important questions to be faced here concerning the definitions of research and its relation to scholarship (a separate and more traditional category) but, as David Marquand forcefully reminded the colloquium, present trends are bringing about a separation between those who research and those who teach without anyone having to do anything to bring it about. The Research Assessment Exercises, in particular, are having the consequence of concentrating research in a clutch of universities, and at the same time separating research staff from those dedicated to teaching within these and other universities. There is even the prospect of a form of disengagement of elements of research activity from universities themselves in the growth of the think-tank and the research and development activity of large corporations, although these tend to remain closely tied to, and even parasitic upon, universities.

## The postmodern university?

Those are some of the ways in which things are changing in the university. Everyone agrees that the growth of mass higher education is an important and valuable phenomenon, but there is an evident fracture between those who interpret these changes as 'postmodern' – as an overturning of what went before, rendering earlier justifications of the university untenable – and those who acknowledge the changes but insist that the continuities remain, together with their established lines of legitimacy. Peter Scott (Chapter 4) tends towards the former view, though he exempts the 'Golden Triangle' of Oxford, Cambridge and London from many of these changes; he documents an association between a post-Fordist economy and a wider postmodern world which has profoundly shaken university life. In this outlook all is change: flexibility, new forms of vocationalism, new forms of pedagogy, new kinds of students, new kinds of learning, a myriad of motives for study, a breakdown of disciplines . . .

But Paul Filmer (Chapter 5) offers a spirited reply to Scott's grand sweep, both querying the conceptual logic of postmodernism and offering a resolute defence of the university as the locus of *disinterested* research, scholarship and teaching. Not insensitive to the realities of change, Filmer's remains an argument that might have been made many years ago in defence of the university ideal.

Perhaps the late Bill Readings (1996, p. 191) best sums up the present challenge to the university:

> An order of knowledge and an institutional structure are now breaking down, and in their place comes the discourse of excellence that tells teachers and students simply not to worry about how things fit together, for that is not their problem. All they have to do is get on with doing what they always have done, and the general question of integration will be resolved by the administration with the help of grids that chart the achievement of goals and tabulate efficiency.

But the university is, has been and can only be a place where thinking is a shared process, where the teaching is part of the unending dialogism of the outer society, 'where thought takes place beside thought'. There must be a future for the university in its work of thinking, which goes on outside the instruction package of corporate excellence, one that has survived the attractions and repulsions of the nostalgic and the romantic.

# Part 1

Postmodernism versus Modernism

# 2

# Universities: Old, New and Different

*Zygmunt Bauman*

## Introduction

According to the *Oxford English Dictionary*, the meaning of the word 'university', agreed no less than nine hundred years ago, is the gathering of teachers and students in pursuit of the higher learning. Much water has flowed under the bridges during those nine centuries, and many bridges have crumbled of old age, or were demolished for their unreliability, while many others, new and improved, have been built. But whatever happens to the water and the bridges, teachers and students go on gathering to pursue higher learning. Obviously they believe, or are led to believe, and believe that this is exactly what is to be believed, that whatever is meant by 'learning' in general and the 'higher learning' in particular, and whatever is seen as worthy of learning, have something in common, something weighty enough to be a good reason to pursue it together, in one building or one set of buildings, under the same authority and according to similar rules and regulations.

Looking back and with the kind of knowledge and understanding available today, one may be excused for suspecting that the belief in question used to be once much better founded than it is now. Indeed, it must have been easier to believe in the common *substance* of learning at the time when it could be neatly compressed into the *trivium*, that threefold road to eloquence, and *quadrium*, that fourfold road to knowledge, or even in the not at all distant times when Ruskin and Dickens felt both competent and obliged to review Mill's *Principles of Political Economy*. It is incalculably more difficult to believe it now, when the incumbents of university offices know little, and comprehend even less, of what their next-door neighbours do in their teaching or research hours, and when they would need a dictionary to understand what the occupants of another floor are talking about, unless the topic of conversation is the thick-headedness of the Registrar's officers, the bloody-mindedness of successive higher education ministers, the short-sightedness of the research-financing committees, the vagaries of the last-generation photocopier, or the deteriorating quality of food in the canteen.

The paucity of inner-university exchange renders also nebulous and irrelevant the once urgent and pregnant issue of a unified and/or unifying scientific *method*. People who rarely talk to each other of the things which matter most to each of them separately are not in the position to judge the similarity or diversity of their actions. Were there one scholarly methodology common to them all, they would hardly notice, and if they did notice it would matter little to most of them, except the philosophers of scientific method – whose method, in turn, matters to no one but themselves.

Perhaps, then, the unity shows itself where teachers meet their students? Perhaps, whatever the teachers teach and the students study, they all agree that there is one way, common to them all, of teaching and studying, transmitting, receiving and appropriating knowledge and skills? A short walk through the lecture theatres and seminar rooms will show the 'teaching method' to be no less a myth than the unified scientific methodology. As Phil Cohen (1995) shrewdly observed,

> lecture styles might run the gamut from charismatic displays of erudition designed to evoke the ghost of some seminal Victorian, or Renaissance polymath, to the impersonal transmission of sound byte sized packets of information in so-called active learning programmes. Seminars might equally be a cross between scholastic disputation and encounter group.

As to the *homines universitatis* who give those lectures and conduct those seminars, one may try, as did for instance Zbigniew Drozdowicz (1995), a Polish historian and sociologist of higher education, to enclose their all-too-evident variety of characters, styles and attitudes into a finite number of types – but only to find out that their list may be extended indefinitely, that idiosyncrasies easily get the upper hand over generalizations, and that the more precisely the types are described the less they fit the fellow academic Peters and Pauls we know.

## Equivalence of classification?

Time and again one discovers, as a tacit rather than outspoken assumption of many collective bargaining positions taken over the years by academic unions, another reason for unity, a democratic idea similar to that of 'one man, one vote': the idea of the essential formal equivalence of skills and know-hows sharply different in substance, and of the substantive neutrality of the criteria by which they can be measured. It does not matter in which section of the university you got your credentials – what does matter is that your examiners recognized them as of first, second or third class, awarded or refused you honours. In the world of education, increasingly ruled by the job market, that formal equality translates into the idea of the equal enabling capacity of similarly marked university degrees and diplomas: whatever your speciality, a first-class degree entitles you to similarly first-class career prospects. Let us note that, in practice, the logic in this reasoning works the other way round: it is the genuine, assumed, and – better still – postulated post-degree equality of treatment and fate that is deployed as the legitimation of the equivalence of the many and varied plots of pre-degree university training and the equality of entitlements of their owners and tillers; if it is true that all graduates are graduates, then it must be true as well that all professors are professors. On the other hand, without the equivalence of graduates, there would be no equivalence of their teachers . . .

This act of faith is buffeted by all sorts of cross-waves. Recently it has been violently brought out of its tranquil, pre-reflexive existence and into the open by the valiant decision to accommodate under one umbrella two systems of higher education of sharply different traditions, recruitment grounds, resource provisions and self-images. I recall this fact not to question that some products of some former polytechnics might have stood head and shoulders above some products of some 'old' universities, but rather to point out that the very idea that an institution may become a university overnight, by administrative decision (and that the decision may be a wholesale one), cannot but prompt much soul-searching regarding the alleged grounds of inner- and inter-university equivalence. We may recall that the recent proliferation of legally sovereign nation-states is a testimony not of the growing number of peoples reaching the demanding conditions of independent existence, but of the watering down and continuous dissolution of the once stern and uncompromising demands of state self-sufficiency and sovereignty.

Other cross-waves are no less testing – for instance, the pressure to work out or impose nationally common standards of teaching and examining which, by the same token, are recognized as not being equal 'naturally' and not having their equivalence guaranteed by anything organically present in the university life as such. Moreover, contrary to its declared motives, the above pressure does not make the word of equality flesh so much as it helps to express in words the all-too-tangible flesh of inequality and, as the inequality goes, acts as a self-fulfilling prophecy. By officially grading the products by the attributes of the factory plant, by giving an a priori stamp of excellence to some trade marks and equally a priori stigmatizing the others, it perhaps makes public knowledge of what used to be a public secret, but in all probability it also makes the new public knowledge into a powerful production tool of privileges and deprivations.

## Shared values?

There is one more line of trenches to which the unity chased away from all other aspects of joint university life may perhaps retire: that of the demarcation and the defence of certain values crucial to the society as a whole, but which need a carefully selected, trained and educated élite to be implemented. Émile Durkheim, as we remember, turned to the university-trained élite searching for the source and the carrier of moral principles in a society hopelessly fragmented by the progressive division of labour and no more capable of generating 'mechanically' the solidarity it needs to live in peace and to survive.

Regarding this proposition, which one would hesitate to reject outright like the others, the following observations can be made. First, the demand for the function in which the universities specialized throughout the modern era, that of the supply of legitimating formula for the up-and-coming modern and modernizing state and the ethical and legal principles of the new and yet untried societal integration, is fast dwindling at a time when the 'primitive accumulation of authority' by the modern state has been successfully accomplished and the emphasis in the meaning of *agora* or *forum* shifts ever more conspicuously from that of the site of public debate to that of the market-place. Second, while remodelling themselves ever more vigorously after the pattern of corporate capital, universities are all too eager, and if not eager then obliged, to cede the right to set the norms, and perhaps most seminally the ethical norms, to its newly embraced prototype and spiritual inspiration. This means stating its own principles ever more gingerly and meekly, and feeling awkward and apologetic whenever those principles clash with the rules sacrosanct to business. Third, rather than attracting their prospective wards with the promise of general wisdom and critical faculty, universities need to undertake the contractual obligation to supply the clients – the consumers of services – with commonly respected certificates of entitlement to such jobs as are currently hoped to secure a decent share in the material or spiritual, but always market-distributed, values. When all three observations are pondered, little credibility is left in the attempt to root the 'unity' bit in the concept of the 'university' in the shared task of value creation and promotion.

## The postmodern condition

One by one, the very old, the less old, and the allegedly brand new contents poured into the concept of the university and justifying the integrity and the uniqueness of the container have been found wanting. Is there any 'common feature' left to the variegated collection of entities called universities, and to the equally variegated interior of any one of them (apart, that is, from the joint legal definition), that upholds the claim of their unity? Or should we rather settle for the much more modest Wittgensteinian idea of a 'family resemblance' only? And should we not seek those resemblances in their diverse, though similarly triggered, responses to the external challenges all those entities and all their fragments face, in the demands raised and the obstacles piled on the way to meeting them – rather than in some obvious or secretive quality of their own?

I suggest that the overwhelming feeling of crisis we all, in a greater or lesser measure, experience, the current version of the 'living at the crossroads' feeling, the feverish search for the new self-definition and, ideally, a new identity as well, have little to do with the faults, errors or neglects of the university academics, but quite a lot to do with the universal melting of identities, dispersal of authorities, and growing fragmentariness of life which characterize the world in which we live – the world I prefer to call 'postmodern', but would not mind being called 'late modern', as Anthony Giddens prefers, 'reflexive modern', as Ulrich Beck does, or even 'surmodern', as George Balandier recently proposed.

The postmodern condition has split one big game of modern times into many little and poorly co-ordinated games, played havoc with the rules of all the games, and shortened sharply the lifespan of any set of rules. Beyond all this slicing and splicing one can sense the crumbling of time, no more continuous, cumulative and directional as it seemed a hundred years ago. Postmodern fragmentary life is lived in an episodic time, and once the events become episodes they can be plotted into history only posthumously; as long as lived, they have only themselves to supply all the sense and purpose they need or are able to muster to keep them on course and to see them through. In such time, the universities, burdened with their sense of history, fit ill and must feel ill at ease. Everything the universities have been doing for the last nine hundred years made sense inside either the time of eternity or the time of progress; if modernity disposed of the first, postmodernity put paid to the second. And the episodic time hovering among the two-tiered ruins of eternity and progress proves inhospitable to everything which we grew up to treat as the mark of the university, that 'coming together in pursuit of higher learning'. Not just to the lifelong academic tenure, but to all those ideas which used to underpin and justify it: that *auspicium melioris aevi*; that experience, like wine, acquires nobility with age; that skills, like houses, are built floor by floor; that reputations can be accumulated like savings and, like savings, yield more interest the longer they are kept.

## I am talked about, therefore I am

Régis Debray (1979) pointed out the gradual, yet relentless, shifting of grounds on which academic reputation, public fame and influence are made and unmade. These grounds used to be the co-operative property of the academic peers, but already in the first half of the twentieth century had been transferred to the management of the publishing houses. The new owners did not manage their property for long, though; it took just a few dozens of years for the grounds to shift again, this time to the ownership of mass media. Intellectual authority, says Debray, was once measured solely by the size of the crowd of disciples flocking in to hear the master; then also, and in a rising degree, by the number of copies sold and critical accolade; but both measurements, though not entirely extinct, have been dwarfed now by television time and newspaper space. For the intellectual authority, the appropriate version of Descartes' *cogito* would be today: I am talked about, therefore I am.

Let us note that this is not just a story of property changing hands and new controllers taking over. The property itself could not emerge unscathed from the change of management, and the shift in control could not but transform the controlled object beyond recognition. Publishing houses cultivate a kind of intellectual authority quite different from that sprouting on university private plots; and the authority emerging of the information-processing plants of the mass media bears but a vague resemblance to either of its two predecessors. According to the witty remark of a French journalist, if Émile Zola were allowed to state his case on television, he would be given just enough time to shout 'J'accuse!'. With public attention turning now into the scarcest of commodities, the media have nothing like the amount of time required to cultivate *fame* – what they are good at is fast-growing and fast-harvested crops of *notoriety*. 'Maximal impact and instant obsolescence', as George Steiner put it, has become the most effective technique of its production. Whoever enters the game of notoriety must play by its rules. And the rules do not privilege the intellectual pursuits which once made the academics famous; the relentless, but slow, search for truth or justice is ill fitted to be conducted under public gaze, unlikely to attract, let alone to arrest, public attention and most certainly not calculated for an instant applause. Once notoriety takes over from fame, college dons find themselves in competition with sportsmen, pop stars, lottery winners, terrorists, bank robbers and mass killers – and in this competition they have little, if any, chance of winning.

## Decline of academic authority

As if this was not strong enough a blow to the status and prestige of the university, the institutionalized institutions of higher education find the once unquestioned right of deciding the canons of professional skill and competence fast slipping out of their hands. At a time when everyone – student, teacher and teacher's teacher alike – has equal access to personal computers connected to the Internet, when the latest thoughts of science, duly bowdlerized, trimmed to the curriculum requirements, user-friendly and tamely interactive, are available in every games shop, while the access to the latest fads and foibles of scholarship depends on money had, rather than the degree held – who then can claim his or her pretence to instruct the ignorant and guide the perplexed to be a *natural* right? The opening of the information superhighway revealed, in retrospect, just how much the claimed, and yet more the genuine, authority of the teachers used to rest on their collective monopoly of the sources of knowledge and the no-appeal-allowed policing of all roads leading to such sources. It also showed to what extent that authority depended on the unshared right of the teachers to decide the 'logic of learning' – the time sequence in which various bits and pieces of knowledge can and need be ingested and digested. With those once exclusive properties now deregulated, privatized, floated on the publicity stock exchange and up for grabs, the claim of academia to be the only and the natural seat for those 'in pursuit of higher learning' sounds increasingly hollow to everybody's ears but those who voice it.

The last rampart of authority may be, perhaps, the exclusive entitlements of the credentials-certifying agency. It is the universities, after all, who remain the sole institutions entitled to encrust the individual know-how with public validity, and thus with an exchange value. Wherever the knowledge came from, it is the legally defined academic outfits which are supposed to examine the results and vouch that it has been duly assimilated and made, indeed, the individual's possession. Erving Goffman pointed out a long time ago that social life would grind to a halt without such institutional confirmation of credentials – a necessary substitute for the personal scrutiny and evaluation of quality, no more a viable prospect amidst the universal otherhood in which we are all cast but in which we need to orient ourselves. Institutional confirmation is not foolproof, but it is the best available protection against the danger of the fakers and false pretenders – a danger as universal as the otherhood itself (if not for the British Medical Association's register, for instance, who would be able to tell a doctor from a quack?).

In this function at least, one could suppose, universities may feel secure. And indeed they might, if not for one circumstance: like all other value-adding monopolies, the monopoly of institutional 'commodification' of acquired or assumed skills also needs a regulated environment to be effective, but the kind of regulation required here, like the tango, takes two. In the case under discussion, the condition of effectiveness is a relatively stable co-ordination between job descriptions and skills descriptions, both relatively stable, at least if measured by the average timespan of the 'pursuit of higher education'. In our increasingly 'flexible' and thoroughly deregulated job market this condition is seldom met, and all prospects of arresting the rot, let alone restoring the rapidly vanishing framework of prospective planning, grow bleaker by the hour. The process of higher learning, historically institutionalized by university practice, cannot easily adopt the job-market pace of flexible experimentation and even less can it accommodate to the all-too-apparent normlessness and thus unpredictability of mutations which the drifting called flexibility cannot but spawn (while the current pressures to enforce uniformity upon variegated curricula and styles of teaching go obviously against the tide and make the challenge of adjustment yet more daunting). Besides, the type of skills required to practise flexible occupations does not, on the whole, demand long-term and systematic learning. More often than not, it transforms a well-profiled, logically coherent body of skills and habits from the asset it used to be into the handicap it now is. And this severely dents the commodity value of the degree certificate. The latter may find it difficult to compete with the market value of on-the-job training, short courses and weekend seminars. The loss of its post-Robbins universal availability and relative cheapness deprived the university education of one more – perhaps even decisive – competitive advantage. With its fast-growing fees and living costs it is not entirely fanciful to suppose that the university education may soon be discovered not offering, in market terms, value for money – and even price itself out of competition altogether . . .

## Postmodern troubles cannot be adequately handled by modern means

Contemporary versions of evolution theory tell us that 'generalistic', that is unchoosy, species have much greater survival capacity than the species splendidly accommodated to a particular ecological niche and thus environmentally selective. It is tempting to say that the universities fall victim to their own perfect fit and adjustment; it just happened that what they adjusted to was a different, now vanishing, world. That was the world marked first and foremost by slow – sluggish by present standards – flow of time. This was a world in which it took quite a while for a spade to stop being a spade, for skills to become obsolete, for specialisms to be relabelled as blinkers, for bold heresies to turn into retrograde orthodoxies, and all in all for the assets to turn into liabilities. Such a world, let me repeat, is now vanishing, and the sheer speed of vanishing is much in excess of the readjustment and redeployment capacity the universities have acquired over the centuries. Besides, it is not just that the situation in which the universities operate is changing; the most difficult thing to cope with adequately is, so to speak, the 'metachange' – the change in the fashion in which the situation is changing . . .

The world an institution adjusts to leaves its imprint on the shape of the institutionalized routine, on the monotony of pattern reproduction. But it also shapes the institution's way of coping with crises, reacting to the environmental change, articulating problems and seeking solutions. Whenever in crisis, and well before the nature of crisis has been fathomed and understood, institutions tend to resort instinctively to the repertory of tried and thus habitualized responses. This is one – the insider's – way of putting it. Another – an outsider's – way would be to observe that crises are joint products of the perception of the situation as critical and proceeding to act in a fashion jarring with what the situation renders possible and/or desirable. What the outsider's perspective reveals, therefore, is the sad yet all-too-real suicidal tendency of any evolutionary success story. The more successful an institution has been in fighting off certain kinds of crises, the less apt it becomes to react sensibly and effectively to crises of a different and heretofore inexperienced kind. I suppose that if applied to the universities this rather banal rule would go some way towards a better comprehension of their present-day predicament, not a small part of which derives from their institutionalized reluctance or learned incapacity to recognize the present environmental change as an essentially novel event – something novel enough to call for a revision of strategic ends and rules of their pursuit.

That the novelty has thus far, by and large, gone unrecognized testifies to the widespread tendency to react to the present challenge in the Habermasian way – that is, through the search for a new consensus and for a new and improved, but once more universally binding, pattern of higher learning. But postmodern troubles cannot be adequately handled with modern means, not necessarily because there is something wrong with those means from the start, but because in the kind of world in which we happen to live now all planning, as Odo Marquand (1987) wittily remarked (paraphrasing Clausewitz's famous adage), is chaos by other means. Whether it would be better if one could impose upon that world a single, ingeniously conceived and painstakingly elaborated, pattern, is not so much dubious as largely beside the point, since the levers capable of lifting such a project are evidently absent, and since all projects lifted with levers of a lesser power invariably augment the dazzling and confusing variety of the hopelessly incoherent and incohesive *Lebenswelt* of postmodern men and women.

I submit that it is precisely the plurality and multi-vocality of the present-day collection of the gatherings 'for the sake of the pursuit of higher learning' – the variety which so jars with the legislators' love of harmony and which they treat therefore with the disgust and contempt due to public threats and personal offences – that offer the universities, old and new and altogether, the chance of emerging successfully from the present challenge. It is the good luck of the universities that there are so many of them, that there are no two exactly alike, and that inside every university there is a mind-boggling variety of departments, schools, styles of thoughts, styles of conversation, and even styles of stylistic concerns. It is the good luck of the universities that despite all the efforts of the self-proclaimed saviours, know-betters and well-wishers to prove the contrary, they are not comparable, not measurable by the same yardstick and – most important of all – not speaking in unison.

Only such universities have something of value to offer to the multi-vocal world of uncoordinated needs, self-procreating possibilities and self-multiplying choices. In the world in which no one can anticipate the kind of expertise that may be needed tomorrow, the dialogues that may need mediation, and the beliefs that may need interpretation (though many do, with consequences ranging from the irrelevant to the disastrous), here the recognition of many and varied ways to, and many and varied canons of, higher learning is the condition *sine qua non* of the university system capable of rising to the postmodern challenge.

Were I making this statement – banal for some, contentious for some others, and horrendous for some others still – hoping for its consensual acclaim or intending to promote a new universal pattern of the academic self-consciousness, I would be denying in deed what I preach in theory. In this chapter there is neither such intention nor such hope. The distinction between 'old' and 'new' universities may soon be smothered by many other criss-crossing and more relevant distinctions, but my sociological conscience would not allow me to suggest that different, inherited and emergent, styles of thinking about universities and their strategies would ever stop to coexist and engage in a battle mutually destructive in its intention yet culturally creative in its consequences. This is, I suppose, how the things here are. And whatever we do, let us start from here.

# 3

# The Need for Place

*Krishan Kumar*

## Loss of justification

Zygmunt Bauman persuasively shows the difficulties of sticking to the old, and the dangers of embracing the new, functions of the university. In a fast-changing society, skills become obsolete before they are fully absorbed; there are no agreed codes of knowledge to be systematically developed and taught; universities no longer have a monopoly (if ever they had) of the skills and knowledge to be passed on to the new generation. At the same time the attempt, in the newer dispensation, to imitate the market and its commercial institutions is bound to end in disaster. Universities possess neither the organizational resources nor the personnel to compete with the much better-equipped and more experienced private commercial organizations. They become absurd and increasingly despised as they compete among themselves like the manufacturers of washing powders, employing increasingly grotesque marketing strategies (see any university promotional video). It is apparent that the fictionalized accounts of current university life, as in Andrew Davies's television series *A Peculiar Practice* or Frank Parkin's novel *The Mind and Body Shop*, have been overtaken by an even more tragically comic reality.

What of the universities' jealously held monopoly of the granting of certificates of quality and eligibility – their right to confer, as Bauman puts it, 'exchange value' on knowledge? Bauman may be right to say that they have a precarious hold on this, in an age of rapidly obsolescent skills and demand for 'flexibility'. This lowers the value of any putative level of skill or knowledge possessed by degree holders. But this has never really been the source of the universities' privileged position in this respect, at least in modern times. Far more important has been the belief that universities selected and developed the right kinds of people, in the sense of people who possess a certain moral character and mental outlook. At what might be considered the peak of the system this was the basis of selection, for instance, of graduates for the old administrative class of the Civil Service, or for general traineeships at the British Broadcasting Corporation. The view was taken that, whatever the subject studied, candidates would have the requisite resources of intelligence and initiative to take on a variety of tasks. If specialized skills or knowledge were required, these were best provided by a combination of practical experience on the job and intensive training courses. In the current environment of rapid skill obsolescence this view seems far more realistic and apposite than the frantic and doomed attempts to make universities mirror the operations and organizational forms of Unilever or Marks & Spencer.

The universities' role in this educative process, it might be relevant to note, has often been misunderstood. The universities were not the makers nor, very much, even the nurturers of the abilities and aptitudes made available to outside institutions. The three years of British undergraduate education are scarcely enough for this. But universities were – and are – unique concentrations of a diversity of talents formed by family, school and class cultures. They provide the milieux in which these talents find the space and opportunity to flourish, often in areas remote from the formal academic curriculum. It is in this, rather than in the provision of formal learning, that the universities are distinctive. It has often struck many of us who work in universities that the students learn more from each other, in a variety of ways, than they do from us: purveyors indeed of increasingly questioned and questionable stocks of knowledge.

If this is so, then it suggests one of the ways in which universities might continue to justify themselves in the age of information. There are indeed many competing sources of information and knowledge. Knowledge itself has indeed become fragmentary, 'timeless values' increasingly contested, pluralism and relativism proclaimed in every sphere. If universities were only about the communication of knowledge or the transmission of imperishable values, then it is difficult to see how they could defend themselves against the charge of being expensive anachronisms. The Open University stands as an admirable model of how whatever counts as knowledge can be disseminated cheaply and efficiently to far greater numbers than are now housed in our conventional universities.

Bauman, rightly I think, rejects this solution. In the face of a 'postmodern' condition he offers a postmodern proposal: let the hundred (or so) varieties of British universities bloom. Do not let governments impose a standard curriculum or a central regulating body. That would kill off the very variety that, in a changing and largely unpredictable environment, allows some – we cannot tell in advance which – institutions and disciplines to nurture relevant and creative kinds of skill and knowledge.

I am sympathetic to this, but feel that it leaves the universities too much hostages to fortune – or, more particularly, to the vagaries of party politics. It endorses the current (though diminishing) variety, but without showing how this can be sustained in the future. The financial and political pressures that universities are currently under make it only too likely that they will imitate each other in pursuing the same strategies of standardization and 'value for money'. This will have the inevitable Darwinian effect of eliminating the unfit, leaving only those best able to exploit the existing political and economic environment – and, presumably, as likely candidates for future extinction as any erstwhile dominant species or variety in the fossil record.

## The importance of place

We need to defend universities – if that is what we wish to do – in terms of what they alone can do, or do best, rather than in terms of what other institutions can do as well or better. If the information society turns everyone into a potential student, with access to knowledge and information on a global scale, then it seems as if universities must emphasize other aspects of their existence than their knowledge-communicating function. Universities are breathing spaces in life's course. They enable their members, young and old, to do things and to reflect on things for which for the rest of their lives they will have neither the time nor the opportunity. This is best done communally, residentially, rather than in the isolation of privatized households. That is why the Open University, excellent as it is in many ways, will not do as a model for universities in general.

One of the current strengths of universities, however dubious the rationale, is that they are virtually the sole accrediting institutions in contemporary societies. It is they alone that give the degrees that, for all but a handful of John Majors and Richard Bransons, are the passports to a reasonably secure and tolerable life. A degree does not guarantee you that security, and these days it does little more than give you a start in life. But that is the point; without a degree you cannot even start, or only with great difficulty and at great risk.

We should make this monopoly our opportunity to re-emphasize and perhaps redefine what universities, and universities alone, are best able to do. The monopoly is indefensible so long as universities see themselves as primarily in the business of imparting knowledge or skills. We may need to keep up this fiction for a while, though it will come to be increasingly transparent before very long. But the real defence of the monopoly, and one that we may have to come clean on in time, is that a degree is given for attendance and participation in a certain sort of cultural and social life. What is now spoken and often thought of as 'extra-curricular' must come to be seen and attended to as the real heart of university life and the main justification of the university's existence.

Universities bring people together. They allow for a cross-fertilization of minds on a scale and in a manner not possible anywhere else in society. Teachers can aid this process; libraries can extend it. But it is the function of teachers and university libraries that is most under threat in the information age. The personal quality of teaching is of course precious, and is one line of defence. But it is no longer as strong a line of defence as it used to be, in these days of mass education and large classes.[1] Moreover, it is not

at all clear that the instruction provided through the new media technologies, especially those involving interactivity, is markedly inferior to that
provided by teachers. As for libraries, for anyone with a personal computer
the best libraries in the world will soon be available to be screen-read at
home. Universities need libraries but libraries do not necessarily need
universities.

## Defending the indefensible?

It has often been said that the function of universities is not to swim with
the tide but to go against it. It is this conviction that underlies the many
accounts of the university that stress its maintenance and enrichment of
a certain high culture against the encroachments of business, politics and
daily life. This was the influential and attractive vision for the universities of
John Henry Newman, Matthew Arnold and F.R. Leavis. Universities are, in
this view, islands of culture and high-minded thought in a sea of commerce
and banality.[2]

This line of defence is no longer tenable. An élitist concept is perfectly
acceptable in an élitist society, when universities are primarily concerned
with educating cultural and political élites. Such is no longer the case in
most contemporary societies. When between a third and a half of the age
cohort go to university, numbers alone speak against this possibility. More to
the point, Bauman is right to say that there is simply no longer a consensus
on what constitutes the high culture, nor agreement that this would be a
desirable aim even if were possible.

That might not matter so much, at least from the point of view of our
present concern, if this applied only to contemporary society and not also
the contemporary university. Universities might then be able to say to society, as of old, 'Go your own (postmodern) way. Let commerce and culture
be one. Unleash the forces of cultural anarchy. We, however, will continue
to insist that there is a high culture; we will cherish the "great tradition",
and seek to transmit it to succeeding generations of students. If they are
more interested in electronic games than great works of literature, this is
regrettable but perhaps not fatal. We, the scholars, will cultivate the great
legacy of the past, and preserve it as best we can until society comes to its
senses.'

Even were this posture politically or economically feasible, it is no longer
a real option. The postmodern turn has, if anything, affected the universities even more than the wider society. It is after all within the academy that
postmodern theory was first formulated, and it is there that it has been
most vigorously elaborated and promoted. The criticisms by different racial,
ethnic and gender groups of the orthodox curriculum, and their demands
for their 'own' studies and departments; the assault by non-Christian religious groups on the predominantly Christian culture of most universities in
the West, and their call for the recognition of the distinctive ways of their

own cultures in the manner and content of what is taught and studied; the principled rejection by many academic theorists in the humanities and social sciences of the very concepts of truth and objectivity that have been the axioms of the rationalist culture of the universities – all these have undermined the concept of a privileged and accepted tradition of high learning that could form the basis of a 'core curriculum' or an agreed body of thought suitable for all students and teachers. There are still valiant efforts to maintain the 'great books' core courses famously instituted by the University of Chicago in the 1930s, but on current showing their future must be very precarious.[3]

But if it is no longer possible to fall back on the defence of universities as the missionary carriers of the high culture, it is still possible to defend them as the sites of cultural exploration and engagement. This takes them beyond the formal teaching function, and beyond the control of teachers and administrators as guardians of truth, taste and standards. There must be teaching, and the research that goes with that; there must be disciplines that mark out the fields of knowledge in various, usually arbitrary, ways. These are the symbolic, one might say, to echo Bagehot, the ceremonial structures that make the real life of the university possible. But a quite inordinate amount of time is spent discussing teaching methods, and an even more inordinate amount of time worrying about the definitions and boundaries of disciplines, and what goes with what in a 'balanced' curriculum. Students learn in spite of teachers, even though they may need teachers as spurs; and disciplines are such accidents of history that it is incredible that anyone can think it is worth defending them in any one form. Let there be teachers and subjects; but let us not take them too seriously, or pretend that the style and the expertise of the one and the carefully assembled programmes of the other really matter to what is of value in the university.

In an information or postmodern age, the university as the privileged disseminator of knowledge is no longer a credible idea. There are too many other contenders and rivals for that role. I would stress the unique nature of the university experience as such. Universities are, or should be, different from other institutions. They should not train future doctors, lawyers, engineers, managers or even professional sociologists or economists – or, at least, not as doctors, lawyers, etc. This should be left to the professional schools and institutes, which are better able to do this, mixing the training where necessary with practical involvement.

## A special place

I want to emphasize the informal side of university life, not as a residual but a central feature of universities. This appears the more so in an age which has seen other institutions take over many of the traditional knowledge-communicating functions. I want to see universities as bright and energetic students of all ages have experienced them at all times: as places to explore themselves with others, in speaking, writing, performing, playing, imagining, stretching themselves in mind and body. Nowhere else, and at no other time in their lives, irrespective of age, will students encounter each other with so much time and so many resources to do so much, unconstrained by the requirements of job or family. The university is indeed a *place*, a physical space with buildings and grounds that exist to facilitate the pursuits of students and teachers. To use them to the full, students need to live there, preferably continuously, over many months and years. No other arrangement can satisfactorily perform this function. That is why the 'home-based university' is virtually a contradiction in terms, as insufficient in its own way as the newer idea of the 'cyberspace' or 'incorporeal' university, linking members through the computerized spaces of the Internet. The privatized university, in which students interact with each other and their teachers though a computer terminal, is all of a piece with the privatized society, the increasing tendency to empty the public spaces of society and to concentrate all activities and involvement in the private space of the home (cf. Kumar, 1997).

William Morris once said that while a man could get as good an education elsewhere as in the University of Oxford – Morris himself learned precious little from his teachers there – there was nowhere else in England where he could get as good an education as in the *city* of Oxford. This seems to me to get to the heart of the matter. Morris was contrasting the purely academic life of Oxford with the education obtained through inhabiting and exploring the countless beautiful buildings – including of course the colleges – in the city, not to mention the countryside surrounding it. It is a contrast that he put to arresting effect in the last section of his utopian romance *News from Nowhere*, where the beauty of the countryside and the buildings bordering the Thames is compared with the emptiness and pedantry that once obtained at the educational institutions that also stood on its banks – notably Eton College and Oxford University (now both happily turned into public libraries open to all). The education that Morris had in mind was the education of the senses and the spirit no less than that of the intellect. For that one needed a special place, with the time to explore it and, no doubt, like-minded people to share in the enterprise (not everyone will find, as Morris did at Oxford, a Burne-Jones and a Faulkner to become lifelong friends and collaborators, but creative people of all kinds have provided plenty of testimony as to the importance of their university days and university friends in forming and stimulating their interests).

I am reminded of Morris's remark at another university, and another place. I have recently moved to the University of Virginia, in the old town of Charlottesville. The University was founded by Thomas Jefferson in the early nineteenth century (it was one of the three things Jefferson wished to be remembered for – the other two did not include twice being president of the United States). Jefferson planned and carefully supervised the construction of his 'academical village', down to the details of student residencies, faculty housing, dining rooms ('hotels') and the gardens and grounds of the campus. From his hilltop home at Monticello a few miles away he could observe with a spyglass the day-by-day work on his university. The result is as satisfying an ensemble as is to be found at any university (or indeed other public) complex: a cascading flow of staff pavilions, student rooms, hotels, alleys and gardens around a colonnaded central lawn, all held in splendid equilibrium by a Palladian rotunda, the original library and focal point of the whole design. Jefferson did not ignore the academic studies to be pursued at the new university. He drew up a curriculum that mixed ancient and modern disciplines, in a humanistic blend that was meant to mirror the Enlightenment philosophy of this, the first secular university in the new republic. But he was clear that the physical design of the university – the varied styles of architecture, the gardens that moved from private retreats for staff into open green spaces for all, the 'hotels' for students and their guests – was itself an essential part of the education offered by the university. By living in such a complex, he said, students would learn 'taste and cultivation'. It was not only to save the Virginia taxpayer customs duty that he labelled the Carrara marble that he imported from Italy to build one of the pavilions 'educational material'.

Whether or not we choose to call our times 'postmodern', it is clear that universities now exist in an environment vastly different from that of the nineteenth century, when the basic idea of the modern university's function was established. Departing in many ways from earlier, medieval ideas, the nineteenth century's view was formed as a reaction to industrialization and modernization. Universities would not oppose these developments, but they would maintain a critical distance from them. It would be their function to preserve the high culture against the onslaughts of modernity – not as an escape from modernity but as a critical engagement with it. It was in this context that Humboldt, Newman and Arnold elaborated their influential accounts of the university's mission.

With further modernization, and with the increasing role particularly of scientific research in economic and technological development, universities were brought more squarely into the centre of society. The walls between the universities and the wider society, it was argued, had to be broken down. It was in this context that one heard the advocacy of such concepts as the 'multiversity'. As Clark Kerr (1963, p. 41), one of its more combative exponents, put it:

The 'Idea of a University' was a village with its priests. The 'Idea of a Modern University' was a town – a one-industry town – with its intellectual oligarchy. 'The Idea of a Multiversity' is a city of infinite variety. Some get lost in the city; some rise to the top within it; most fashion their lives within one of its many subcultures. There is less sense of community than in the village but also less sense of confinement. There is less sense of purpose than within the town but there are more ways to excel. There are also more refuges of anonymity – both for the creative person and the drifter. As against the village and the town, the 'city' is more like the totality of civilization as it has evolved and more an integral part of it; and movement to and from the surrounding society has been greatly accelerated.

Kerr's concept of the multiversity, despite its dismissal by contemporary radicals as a time-serving capitulation to government and big business, is actually quite a good description of what in fact happened to universities in the decades following the Second World War. Universities, having for much of the time kept their distance from society, were drawn into the hurly-burly of everyday political and economic life. Academics became advisers to governments and business corporations, researchers engaged in large-scale projects that were meant to advance the purposes of grant-givers from both these spheres. The university, especially in its research function, came to seem essential to the further progress of advanced industrial societies. It was in this climate that sociologists such as Daniel Bell advanced the idea of the university as the central institution of the emerging 'postindustrial society'.

We can see now that this involvement of the universities with contemporary political and economic institutions has, ironically, destroyed not only their traditional aloofness but also much of their recently gained relevance to those very institutions that they we were so anxious to serve. The post-industrial society, in its later post-Fordist, postmodernist phase, has brought about developments that have undermined the universities' privileged position as the creators of new knowledge and the power-centres of training and research. Universities now have to compete with an increasing range of specialized organizations that, based on the new information technologies and with a more precise brief, can offer equally good or better services to government and business.

This is why universities must cease to ape other organizations and purposes and concentrate on what they are still best at providing. In an increasingly home-based, privatized society, universities are among the few surviving institutions that draw people out of their private spaces and, for a brief but crucial time, encourage them to engage in shared public activity. In this sense universities need once more to insist on their difference from the rest of society. It is not the kind of difference the nineteenth century had in mind. But perhaps Newman, Arnold and the others had the right instinct in urging universities not to bow to contemporary demands but to follow their own path. In the end, as they also believed, society will come to see that in this way it too is best served.

## Notes

1. 'Since the majority of undergraduates in the world today have never experienced anything remotely resembling sustained personal attention, the impersonality of machine learning seems almost normal' (Rothblatt, 1996).

2. This conception of the university's function is reiterated at regular intervals; see, for example, Minogue (1973) and, less conservatively, Barnett (1990). It is a conception, it should be noted, directly related to the age of industrialism – previous centuries took for granted the training function of universities, though perhaps preparation for service to the church or state involved a wider conception of education than training accountants and marketing executives.

3. America is as always more advanced than, say, the UK in all this – see the papers in the Fall 1993 issue (vol. 122, no. 4) of *Daedalus* on 'The American Research University', especially those by Neil Smelser and John Searle. The difficulties of establishing and defending a curriculum based on the rationalist tradition do not mean that one cannot be attempted, nor justified.

# 4

# The Postmodern University?

*Peter Scott*

## Introduction

One approach to understanding the university today is to start with general, even sublime, questions and end with particular, perhaps banal, issues and policies. Such questions are readily available, even if answers are more elusive. The first, and a natural starting-point, concerns the characteristics of knowledge in a postmodern world – if that it not an oxymoron because 'characteristics' suggest regularity in an increasingly chaotic intellectual culture. Paradoxically the more closely the 'knowledge' society is approached, the more problematical, contested and elusive knowledge seems to become. A second sublime question, and the most logical next step in an ordered argument, is the role of intellectuals, always an 'iffy' category in atheoretical Britain – or, more fairly, England; George Davie's 'democratic intellect' in Scotland is not entirely a sentimental myth (Davie, 1961; 1986). Intellectuals are a key group in the context first of the professionalization, or now perhaps the deinstitutionalization, of 'knowledge'. A third big question concerns the interventions of universities in, or their dissociation from, public policy debates, another climacteric topic because only in the past generation, and notably during the Thatcher period, has the traditional balance between the autonomy of the universities and their élite complicity, or conformity, been upset. They now face substantially increased political risks as they have to refashion their critical engagement with public policy – and confront the power of fractious élites.

The fourth question concerns the relationship between higher education and the economy. Always latently dominant, this is now seen as the key determinant of the university's future development. Today it is expected to create not only cultural capital but also economic wealth, and as global competitiveness has superseded military rivalry as the measure of national success, higher education has become a key arena. A fifth, rather less grand question concerns 'graduateness', the qualities we expect from, or require of, university graduates. Here the consequences of democratization, with its less rigorous skills regime, seem to be in conflict with the imperatives of hyperprofessionalization and upskilling (but also, paradoxically, demand for labour-market flexibility and skills adaptability).

This approach, beginning with normative principles and descending to operational outcomes, appears unimpeachable logically – but all logical linear flows are now suspect. An alternative approach is possible according to which all these elements – epistemological, sociological, economic, political, technological – are intertwined. The epistemology of the modern university does not determine its sociology; nor the other way round. Rather their relationship, and of the other elements, is one of dynamic reflexivity. The elusive contours of (postmodern?) knowledge; the constitution of the mass university; the transformation of academic work; the 'flight' of intellectuals from higher education to the mass media; new articulations between education, skills and employment; the changing nature of the student experience – all these are linked phenomena that cannot be graded either causally or even hierarchically.

Like all the best arguments, the argument in this chapter is divided into three parts. First, the radical transformation of the university in terms of both its sociological base and academic culture has to be considered; in a (too?) simple phrase, mass higher education. This has led to a far-reaching, if poorly articulated, shift in our notions of 'graduateness'. Next, the equally radical changes in society and the economy need to be discussed; in an equally treacherous phrase, post-Fordism and all that. Arguably the transformation of the university is merely one of these changes, a key component in the multiple modernizations of the late twentieth-century world (Scott, 1995). As a result, the market for high-level skills, and also for 'expert' professional knowledge, has been transformed. Finally, the joint impact of both phenomena, mass higher education and post-Fordism, on what is expected and/or required of graduates in the next millennium has to be assessed.

## Mass higher education

The claim that Britain has acquired a mass system of higher education remain contested. Sceptics point to the exclusion of the majority of young people. Although overall participation is now almost one in three, only a quarter of school leavers go to universities or other higher education institutions. They also argue that the expansion of student numbers that began in the second half of the 1980s, and led to a near-doubling in the size of the system, was curtailed in the early 1990s by the new policy of 'consolidation'. In that sense normality has been resumed. They argue further that, however impressive this quantitative expansion, it has not been accompanied by a qualitative transformation of fundamental academic values or institutional instinct (Wagner, 1995). The exceptionalism of British, or at any rate English, higher education, rooted in notions of intimacy, pastoral and intellectual, that reflect the collusive class-bound clubbability of our national culture, is still intact – just.

Yet, suggestive as such arguments are, the contrary evidence is more persuasive. There are five respects in which the massification of the British system can be demonstrated. The first is the scale of recent expansion. The age participation index has increased from 17 per cent in 1987 to 32 per cent in 1995. According to the most popular taxonomy of higher education systems they cease to be élite systems when they enrol more than 15 per cent of the eligible population and become 'universal' systems when they enrol more than 40 per cent (Trow, 1973). In barely a decade British higher education has moved from being a still recognizably élite system to become a system that is fast approaching the 'universal' threshold. Because wastage remains comparatively low by international standards, Britain now produces more graduates annually than either France or Germany. Claims that the British system is substantially more selective academically, socially restrictive and numerically underdeveloped than higher education systems in other advanced countries can no longer be sustained.

A number of important consequences have flowed from this expansion of higher education, and the step-change it has produced. One is that the incestuous links between participation in an élite system and access to élite occupations have been eroded, although the mass production of graduates and the actual stratification of a formally undifferentiated system have probably strengthened the market position of graduates from the remaining élite institutions (Brown and Scase, 1994). This change will be discussed in greater detail later. Another consequence is that the 'positional' advantages once conferred by a higher education have been much reduced. This change has both intensified, and weakened, the functionalism of the system and instrumentalism of students. As 'positional' advantage has weakened, the contest for residual competitive advantage has sharpened. And, again, the general effect is highly differentiated by institutional hierarchy. A further consequence is that 'over-production' of graduates is no longer a distant and implausible prospect. Despite the rhetorical advocacy of even higher levels of participation by the Confederation of British Industry, the Council for Industry and Higher Education and other economic pressure-groups, there is clear evidence that the traditional market for graduates is now saturated. As a result the graduate jobs market is being radically revised.

The second respect in which the massification of British higher education is demonstrated is the sharp reduction in unit costs. Overall productivity gains of more than 25 per cent have been achieved since 1990 (Watson, 1996). This pattern, which exactly matched the expansion of student numbers, closely follows the cost curves in other countries where mass higher education systems developed earlier than in Britain. It supports the claim that mass systems have a quite different economy from that of élite systems. Although the persistence (even reinforcement) of élite institutions within mass systems means that cost reductions are unlikely to imposed even-handedly across the whole system, the particular arrangements for funding

British higher education have made it difficult for the best universities to defend their historic differentials (and so, they would argue, their ability to compete with their international peers).

Although inadequately researched, the impact of this change on academic and institutional cultures has been profound. As a result of productivity gains there has been a significant intensification of the academic labour process which, combined with new pressures to be more productive in research, has made it especially difficult to maintain the intimate traditions of British higher education. Attachment to these traditions, in turn, has made it more difficult in British universities and colleges than in some other systems to adapt to these changes, although it can be argued that the main burden of the productivity gains has been borne by those institutions least attached to these traditions. The tangible effects of this labour intensification have been a sharp rise in staff–student ratios and often enforced moves towards student-directed learning and self-assessment; its intangible effects probably include an attenuation of personal relationships between students and teachers and among academic colleagues and their substitution by bureaucratic systems of counselling, guidance, quality assurance and so on, leading arguably to an erosion of the idea(l) of an academic community.

The third respect in which the massification of British higher education is demonstrated is a step-change institutional scale. Once universities with more than 10,000 students were rare. Larger institutions, unless subdivided into smaller units (whether Oxbridge-style colleges or constituent colleges within federal universities), were regarded as inimical to the development of an appropriate pastoral regime for students, collegiality among academic staff, and the low-intensity management that was the best defence of institutional autonomy and academic freedom. When in the early 1960s the Robbins Committee recommended that higher education be expanded (Committee on Higher Education, 1963), it was axiomatic that the bulk of this expansion should be achieved by establishing new universities or developing existing further education colleges. Significantly the most recent, and more radical, phase of expansion required the creation of no new institutions. Instead existing institutions expanded their student numbers. As a result, several British universities approach, or exceed, 20,000 students. Although still on the small side by the standards of those in other mass systems, British institutions have ceased to be exceptional in this respect (and further institutional rationalization, although temporarily in abeyance, cannot be ruled out).

The emergence of much larger institutions has had two effects. One has been to compound the first two changes – the widening of access and the reduction in unit costs. Students, increasingly drawn from heterogeneous (and non-élite) backgrounds, are now taught in mass universities for less money, both of which characteristics sharply reduce the possibility of maintaining the old academic culture. As a result, essentialist demarcations, once between universities and other higher education institutions and now between higher education and other forms of education, both of which depended to a significant degree on the maintenance of this traditional culture, have been eroded. This, too, is characteristic of mass higher educa- tion in which essentialist (as opposed to functionalist) categories are typically anachronistic. The other effect is that the acceptance of, even enthusiasm for, much larger universities, and corresponding feelings of vulnerability experienced in smaller colleges, reveal a significant shift in institutional cultures. The ideal of community has been downgraded along with attach- ment to collegiality because neither can easily survive in mass institutions. Conversely, the profile and power of institutional managers have increased because larger institutions demand an enhanced management capacity. Again this is characteristic of mass higher education systems.

The fourth respect in which the massification of British higher education is demonstrated is the existence of a unified system that, politically and organizationally, is undifferentiated but in practice is stratified by the opera- tion of various markets, some rooted in traditional hierarchies of esteem but others more dynamic in character. This unified system was established as a result of the 1992 Further and Higher Education Act that 'promoted' the polytechnics to university status and created a common administrative structure and funding system for the enlarged university and residual college of higher education sectors. (Separate, but similarly unified, systems were established in Scotland and Wales.) At first sight the association between unified and mass systems is weak. Many mass systems, notably the American, are formally differentiated into separate institutional levels. (This is true of nearly all state systems; private institutions are informally stratified by prestige.) In continental Europe binary systems, with a clear demarcation between universities and higher vocational education, typically survive.

However, these other mass systems were established when centralized plan- ning of higher education was still prevalent. In contrast, mass higher edu- cation in Britain emerged more recently when faith in planning had been sharply reduced and greater reliance came to be placed on the operation of the market. Similar trends can now be observed in other national systems where the state has devolved power to universities, curtailing the role of planning agencies and co-ordinating bodies and (by accident or design) encouraging competition among institutions. Sweden and the Netherlands are perhaps the best examples of these experiments in devolution, and in some American states there has been a retreat from state-wide co- ordination of higher education (often to free flagship state universities to compete more effectively with private institutions). In this respect, differ- entiation by the market rather than stratification by planning, the British system is probably a trend-setter rather than a laggard.

The combined effects of creating a unified system and encouraging a market orientation have produced a number of important consequences. One has been to stimulate a spirit of competition among universities, a rivalry that has outstripped in intensity the actual competitive requirements imposed by the funding system. A significant shift in corporate mental- ity seems to have taken place. Its most blatant manifestation is the rise of marketing (Smith *et al.*, 1995). Another consequence, closely linked to the first, is the drive to identify discrete markets, and to occupy favourable market niches, now that a fixed hierarchy of institutional roles has been formally abandoned. A third, also closely linked, is the desire to make institutions as attractive as possible to potential students, now generally reconceptualized as 'customers'. Customer choice now rivals academic selection as a determinant of access to higher education. A fourth consequence is a new emphasis on improved performance, because in a unified/market system budgets depend on compliance with quasi-contracts (and so are output-related) rather on the roll-over of existing funding levels (generally based on historic inputs). From an institutional perspective the overall effect has been to produce greater volatility. For students it has been to produce a plurality of institutions, no longer conveniently categorized but nevertheless increasingly differentiated.

The fifth and final respect in which the massification of British higher education is manifest is the undermining of traditional 'scientific' culture, not simply in terms of the decay of cultural-intellectual 'canons' that reflected the interests and aspirations of an élite student body but also in terms of growing scepticism about the claims of universalism made on behalf of the values of cognitive rationality. This double erosion has many sources – the accumulation of epistemological doubts, at their most dramatic in the postmodern movement but more banally pervasive; the perceived inadequacy of reductionist scientific techniques to cope with phenomena such as risk; the desire to produce a more 'relevant' higher education for students now drawn from more heterogeneous constituencies; a similar emphasis on scientific applications and on the contextualization of knowledge (Gibbons *et al.*, 1994); the general retreat of élite culture before the advance of populism. Generally such cultural, intellectual and scientific phenomena are not linked to the growth of mass higher education. But there are obvious affinities, and even some closer-to-causal connections, between them and the sociological opening-out of the modern university.

There are even more intriguing affinities between this deconstruction of traditional 'scientific' culture (in the fullest sense: its cognitive values, social practices and institutional forms) and the emergence of what is termed a 'knowledge' society. According to the standard, but perhaps superficial, account, the development of a society in which class- or gender-based stratification is gradually being superseded, or at any rate modified, by differentiation by accreditation and of an economy in which codified knowledge is becoming a primary resource is likely to enhance the role and prestige of 'knowledge' institutions, among which the universities are arguably preeminent. But according to an alternative, and perhaps more subtle, account the growth of a 'knowledge' society is associated with two phenomena, both more problematical from the universities' point of view. The first is the emergence of new kinds of 'knowledge' institutions, that are not characterized by the same patterns of academic and professional socialization as the universities and which apparently offer a rival model. The second is that 'knowledge', conceptually and operationally, has become a much more capacious category; it has spread far beyond academic and/or scientific definitions.

It is no longer clear that universities, as currently (or foreseeably) constructed, are best able to generate and manipulate these new forms of socially distributed knowledge. (These forms extend far beyond 'applied' science or technology 'transfer'; such archaic vocabulary represents an anachronistic account of knowledge production.) Knowledge is no longer privileged, in the sense that its reproduction is restricted to an academic (and social?) caste. Nor is it 'expert', in the sense that reductionist techniques are indubitably the most effective. As a result, universities, in the new mass age, are less able to guarantee students access to a privileged body of knowledge, because such a body of knowledge no longer exists, or to socialize them into 'expert' niches within a carefully differentiated division of professional labour, because that division of labour has been eroded from 'within' by epistemological insecurity and from 'without' by the reconfiguration of the labour market.

## Post-Fordism and all that

The growth of mass higher education is not an isolated phenomenon. It is one aspect of much wider, and deeper, transformation of the late modern world. And that transformation has radically reshaped what can be expected of graduates and, more important, what they expect of higher education. Two broad-brush accounts of these changes are available. The first is most conveniently labelled postindustrialism. It is rooted in technological determinism. Innovation and productivity are the key to step-changes, or 'waves' (currently the fifth wave). 'Knowledge' – by which generally is meant information technology – is seen as the fundamental resource of late twentieth-century society, just as oil was in the mid-twentieth century and coal and steel in the Victorian age. Social change is subordinate. For example, two highly respected science policy analysts in a recent article argued that the Fifth Wave, the triumph of micro-electronics, demanded 'a full-scale reaccommodation of social behaviour and institutions' (Freeman and Perez, 1988, p. 59). Also change is essentially linear. The teleological ghost is still in the machine.

The best shorthand title for the second account is post-Fordism (Amin, 1994). This suggests more than simply a shift in the dominant mode of production, the result of a quantum leap in innovation-induced productivity. Rather it suggests an accumulation of abandonments – of undifferentiated mass production, of linear careers (indeed of 'work'), of hierarchical (and deferential) social structures, even of personal identities as traditionally determined. Or, to put it another way, changes in the regime of accumulation are subordinate to changes in the mode of political, social and cultural regulation. Post-Fordism is as much a cultural as an economic phenomenon.

It lacks regularity; indeed, it is wide open to regression. And, while the relationship between industrial and postindustrial society is essentially linear, that between Fordist and post-Fordist regimes is dialectical.

The choice between these two accounts can be reduced to a simple question: continuity – or, at any rate, a linear sequence of 'waves' – or rupture, dislocation, non-sequential novelty? Five fundamental attributes of contemporary society can be identified which, on balance, tend to support rupture rather than continuity, post-Fordism rather than postindustrialism:

1. *Acceleration.* Not simply the exponential growth of almost everything, goods and services, data and images, which apparently only the most powerful computers can regulate; but, alongside velocity, volatility. Nothing, it seems, is for ever – or for very long. Lyotard (1984a) has written, revealingly, of 'the temporary contract supplanting permanent institutions' – in politics, culture, the economy, intellectual life, social affairs, even the most intimate personal relationships.
2. *Time-space.* Radical new compressions (and conceptions) of time-space, which have been labelled 'simultaneity', or 'uchronia' now that utopias are no longer available (Nowotny, 1994). This is revealed by ungainly new coinages such as 'glocalisation' (Featherstone *et al.*, 1995). One effect is the intensification of time, whether in the labour process or consumption patterns. Another is the urge to resist this intensification, by formulating a new 'ecology' of time-space.
3. *Risk.* The gain in power produced by technological (and, for 'wave' enthusiasts, economic) progress is increasingly undermined by the accumulation of risks (Beck, 1992). 'Risk' considerations can no longer be regarded as side-effects. Unintended 'risks' shape social action as decisively as intended outcomes, whether political reforms or technical innovations.
4. *Complexity, non-linearity, circularity.* Really a bundle of attributes. The first is familiar enough – and, arguably, able to be controlled by developing more sophisticated models of chaos theory and building more powerful computational systems to handle enormous data sets. The second is mirrored in the popularity of more 'open' and fluid accounts of social, economic, technical change in preference to rationalistic, mechanistic, positivistic 'equilibrium' models. Circularity, of course, is most apparent in the social sciences, where 'social' knowledge 'grows' through interaction with its environments.
5. *Reflexivity.* This takes several forms. One is the democratization (and marketization) of knowledge production and innovation systems which were briefly referred to at the end of the first section of this chapter, in the sense that 'subjects' and 'objects' of enquiry or action become jumbled up. Another is that, as expert and abstract systems take over from traditional structures, both values and institutions are freed from the fixities, or givens, of tradition. Instead they must be constructed, and frequently reconstructed, in the light of interaction between these

expert systems and actual environments. A third is that, as traditional class, gender and other distinctions fall away, individuals are freer to write their biographies. In Ulrich Beck's (1992, p. 90) phrase, 'the individual becomes the reproduction unit of the social'.

It is against this background that the more detailed socio-economic trends of our times – one of which, of course, is the growth of mass higher education – must be considered. These trends include the 'death' of the welfare state; the rise of the so-called 'audit society'; the accelerating shift from manufacturing to services (and the tendency for these services to be concerned with the high-velocity delivery of symbolic goods); the death of 'work', at least in the sense that bureaucratic careers are replaced by job 'portfolios'; the transformation of production through customization, just in time and so on (and the parallel transformation of organizations as outsourcing and rightsizing have their effect). And these socio-economic changes have been accompanied by profound cultural effects. Two in particular are worth mentioning. First, where a generation ago a tension was discerned between global capitalism and mass culture, between the regulation of production and the recklessness of consumption, today the synergy between them is more likely to be emphasized. Playfulness now produces profit; images (and ideas) are commodities. In short, superstructure is now structural. Second, a far-reaching individualization is under way. Lifestyles, as realized through personal participation in consumption, are now perhaps more fundamental determinants of personal identity and social hierarchy than life chances, as determined by one's place in the division of labour or conventional social hierarchy. Biographies have truly become reflexive, chosen as well as given.

## Tomorrow's graduates

The graduates of the future will have experienced a new kind of higher education, and come from and go into a new kind of society. Both will be, or already are, radically different from the standard twentieth-century models, the meritocratish élite higher education that emerged as a result of the Robbins expansion and the polytechnic project and the urban, industrial, bureaucratic, welfare state that so decisively shaped personal aspirations, social expectations and economic patterns during the two post-1945 generations. Mass higher education and post-Fordist society are less the linear successors of these earlier forms than their dialectical challengers. Many of the key assumptions made in élite higher education systems (for example, notions of academic excellence validated by selective entry or the intimate, even incestuous, association between graduate status and access to élite occupations) no longer apply in mass systems. Similarly, fundamental assumptions about the character of the industrial welfare state (for example, a progressive social order underpinned by fullish employment, stable career patterns and a comprehensive social security system, all requiring the maintenance of a substantial public sector to compensate for the volatility and inequity of private markets) have been challenged.

As a result the expectations that universities can have of their students and, more significantly, the expectations that students have of higher education, are undergoing radical changes. There is much evidence of this already – the Higher Education Quality Council's (HEQC) (probably vain) attempt to define 'graduateness'; the deprofessionalization and parallel bureaucratization of quality assurance; arguments about modularization, semesterization and credit accumulation and transfer; the foregrounding of competence-denominated skills; the growing fuzziness between 'higher' and other forms of post-school education (including corporate training); concern about the expansion of franchising, validation and other forms of accreditation (for example, of work-based learning); fears about the incorporation of higher education, with its strong professional and public service ethic, within the burgeoning infotainment industry with its unrestrictedly commercial orientation.

Graduate expectations and/or requirements will be framed by four broad trends that reflect the growth of mass higher education and development of a post-welfare state and post-Fordist society. The first is volatility and ephemerality. This has several aspects. One is the impact of technological (and social) acceleration; another is the process of deinstitutionalization, whether this takes the form of the development of 'virtual' institutions or the deconstruction of large bureaucracies and their replacement by flexible organizations; a third is the growth of 'local knowledges', a plethora of knowledge traditions that ebb and flow; and a fourth is the trend away from permanent institutions and towards temporary contracts in everything from grand public bodies to intimate personal relations. Acceleration and ephemerality mean that graduates will have to be educated in novel ways. It is not simply a question of providing them with the skills of lifelong learning – curiosity, flexibility and adaptability – but of encouraging the development of a new mentality that is ironic, intuitive and 'instantaneous'.

The second trend is towards a new articulation between higher education and the labour market. This, too, is a product of technological acceleration which dramatically curtails the currency of high-level skills and expert knowledge. It is reflected also in the decline of large-scale bureaucratic organizations, in the private as well as the public sector, that typically employed large numbers of graduates. Yesterday's (and today's?) graduates were socialized into a rationalistic, progressive and 'bureaucratic' jobs culture. Tomorrow's graduates will have to be socialized into a new jobs culture, because their occupational destinations will be much more diverse and diffuse. Finally, and more fundamentally, this new, and perhaps fuzzier, relationship between higher education and employment is an aspect of the deeper disarticulation of professional society. Again, the impact on values may be greater than on careers. Many key values, whether the public service, scientific or even the Smilesian self-improvement ethic, developed within the context of the professional society that grew up in the later nineteenth and twentieth centuries. If that form of society is to be eroded in the twenty-first century, these normative structures are likely to be increasingly challenged. Graduates, once the most important transmitters of these professional values, will be required to make radical adjustments – of mood and mentality as well as of their occupational formation.

The third trend is towards marketization. Often markets are regarded as procedural rather than moral arenas. But the message of their intrusion into higher education is unlikely to be lost on students. Two aspects in particular deserve to be emphasized. The first is that the essence of a university education, its magic, is likely to be eroded as higher education is increasingly incorporated in a larger leisure-and-learning sector which, according to the recent Technology Foresight exercise that created this omnibus category, now accounts for 13 per cent of the gross national product (Office of Science and Technology, 1995). The second is that marketization suggests that there are no longer any unified subjects, reserved areas protected from the transgression of commercial transactions (Eagleton, 1994). Through their redesignation as customers, students are both empowered, because their immediate demands are more likely to be satisfied, and diminished, because their longer-term needs may be ignored and their participation in a symbolic, transcendental, even magical, experience will be denied.

The fourth, and final, trend is towards new forms of credentialization that will drive lifestyles as well as life chances. This also has two aspects. The first is that, as older forms of social stratification, based on class and gender, race and place, decline in importance because of consumerist individualization, newer forms of differentiation are likely to emerge. Being a graduate is likely to be one of these. Increasingly graduate status will be the principal signifier of cultural capital. Put simply, it will be (perhaps is) no longer possible to be middle-class without going into higher education. Universities will produce, not simply reproduce and reflect, social hierarchies. And students, by participating in higher education, will be able to construct their own reflexive biographies. The second aspect is that, as 'work' in a traditional sense shrinks, individuals will seek alternative indicators of their worth and status. Again participation in higher education may come increasingly to provide these alternative indicators. It is possible to see this shift from defining social identities in terms of occupational hierarchy to defining them in terms of academic 'ranks' as a reversion to older, pre-industrial and pre-professional, stratification. But it also has more progressive and radical implications. Already, many women, traditionally disadvantaged in (or excluded from) formal labour markets, have turned to higher education to construct alternative identities.

The impact of these trends on the university curriculum, in its widest sense, will be profound. It will have to reflect the new vocationalism which is very different from older forms of professional and vocational education. Because 'content', in terms of authoritative knowledge traditions, and 'expertise', in the shape of organized and specific high-level skills, will become less important, and because the complicit, even collusive, culture of élite higher education, which was able to define and refine future élites by reference to implicit values and silent prejudices, has been increasingly challenged by the more open culture of mass higher education, aptitudes and attitudes now have to be explicitly developed. This helps to explain the growing emphasis on 'competences', the pressure to articulate aims and objectives and to identify learning outcomes. Similarly the sociological diversity of those who now participate in higher education, combined with the epistemological erosion of authoritative knowledge traditions, has led to the re-emergence of 'local knowledges'. This has reshaped power relationships within the learning environment. Finally, because higher education is no longer necessarily a preliminary to 'work' (and to the social participation it affords) but, sometimes, an antidote to it and even, in the symbolic society of the future, reconfigured 'work', social participation in its own right, universities will need to pay more attention to the development of social and life skills in their graduates, perhaps at the expense of the élite and/ or expert formation that has been their main business for much of the twentieth century.

# 5

# Disinterestedness and the Modern University

*Paul Filmer*

## Forms and ideas of the modern university

Since the end of the Second World War and the sense of social reconstruction that it precipitated, there has been much debate about the several ideas, especially as ideals, of the university in Britain. One consequence of this is a growing difficulty in sustaining a unitary – or even a coherent – concept of the institution. This is especially so in the face of recent and current changes in the structure and funding of contemporary universities in all developed societies. The process has been termed one of transition from élite to mass higher education (Parsons and Platt, 1973; Meyersohn, 1975; Scott, 1995) and it is one which is not only producing changes in the functions of universities; inevitably it is calling into question the character of the university itself as a social institution in ways that have already begun to necessitate major changes in its structural forms. I want to begin, therefore, by identifying the main ideas of the modern university in terms of the structural forms that these have taken.

There is, first, the idea promulgated by F.R. Leavis (1948; 1969) that the university is essential to the preservation of the culture of the minority in the face of mass civilization. This implies an ideal of the university which belongs in a tradition that dates back to the arguments, in the second half of the nineteenth century, of Newman (1987) on the role of the modern university and Arnold (1983) on the threats of modern society to traditional literary culture. It is an ideal which is tied unequivocally, in Leavis's formulation, to an institutional form and intellectual commitments based on the Oxbridge model. What it excludes is as important as what it represents:

> The university, in so far as it is more than a centre and nursery of the sciences, a technological institute, or a collocation of specialist departments, is the ... organ through which society has to make the sustained effort (one directed by collaborative intelligence and a full human

responsibility) to . . . provide our civilization with memory and mature purpose.

(Leavis, 1969, p. 58)

Such a concept of the university, acting as

a centre of consciousness for the community must have its centre in an English school . . . a focus of cultural continuity can only be in English. . . . There is no other access to anything approaching a full continuity of mind, spirit and sensibility.

(Leavis, 1969, pp. 59–60)

As a project, this version of the university has failed, notwithstanding the continuing survival – albeit compromised by the incorporation of science centres, technological institutes and specialist departments – of the ancient collegiate universities on which it was based. Indeed, such universities for a time provided a model of one form of development of British higher education at the beginning of the second half of the twentieth century. The ideal was to preserve the continuity of a cultural tradition whose life depends upon the survival of a meritocratically élite intellectual minority; yet the model offered as best suited to provide for this showed an alarming sociological naïvety in ignoring its functionality for the reproduction of what Eliot (1948) termed, considerably less meritocratically, 'high culture'. Though Leavis, unlike Eliot, insists that this high culture is not antipathetic to industrial society, it is nevertheless related closely to what Wiener (1981) has identified as the decline of the industrial spirit in England – a pre-Raphaelite neo-medievalism characteristic of late nineteenth-century thought in Britain and not unrelated to the physiocratic reaction to early modern European society. The humanist idealism of this ethos continues to penetrate contemporary debates about the idea of the university.

Second, there is the nineteenth-century metropolitan university of London, and its provincial colleges which were chartered into autonomy as universities in the decade following the end of the Second World War. The idea underlying them grew out of Bentham's founding of University College London, and carried, inevitably, a flavour of these origins in utilitarian thought. It was of a modern university, appropriate to the conditions and concerns of a new industrial bourgeois society, in contrast with the essentially medieval, pre-modern Oxbridge model. The epistemological and cultural ideal was to embrace the applied as well as the pure sciences, the study of political economy and the social sciences as well as the classics and humanities. This provoked an engagement with the traditional culture that was made public in the so-called 'Two Cultures debate', constructed out of a series of otherwise unremarkable exchanges between Leavis and C.P. Snow in the 1960s. The issues to which Leavis and Snow alluded were addressed more effectively by the New Left in Britain (see Anderson, 1968; Mulhern, 1979), and have since become a cornerstone of the controversial discourses of cultural studies (see Hall, 1980; Davies, 1993). This controversy is an invariable marker of one form of objection to the massification of higher education, and of the economic relevance of a university degree in the post-industrial, post-Fordist and postmodern complex of contemporary social and cultural environments (see, for example, Scott, 1995; Phillips, 1996).

Third, there is the idea of the university which is tied to the ideal of the white-hot mid-century technological revolution that underwrote the Labour Party's 1964 election campaign and was implicit in some of the recommendations of the Committee on Higher Education (1963) headed by Lord Robbins. This led, first, to the translation to chartered university status of several degree-awarding institutions that had been termed colleges of advanced technology. These institutions were essentially centres for the study of the applied sciences and their technological application. They sought to consolidate the ideal of the metropolitan university by complementing their focus on technology with a rational scientific humanism, usually by creating departments of social science. At the same time, a number of new, ex-urban campus universities were established, most of which were modelled on the Oxbridge, collegiate residential style. These 'plateglass' universities,

> despite their self-conscious modernity, largely expressed in a great emphasis on the social sciences, . . . by and large shared Oxbridge's lack of interest in technology and business . . . were located away from large centers of population, in the cathedral town-country estate setting that had become typical of elite schools. In these cases, physical form followed social and psychological function – the embodiment of an ideal of 'civilization' bound up with preindustrial, preurban models – forming an amalgam of an idealized medieval church and a similarly idealized eighteenth-century aristocracy.
>
> (Wiener, 1981, p. 23)

Fourth, there are the new universities, created by the 1992 legislation which sought to unify the binary system. This brought into the university sector the large polytechnics which had developed a significant collective identity during the late 1960s and early 1970s, as a further part of the post-Robbins expansion of higher education. As well as the traditional range of academic provision, they offer an eclectic mixture of professional and vocational courses, of varying duration and providing a variety of sub-degree, degree-equivalent and postgraduate qualifications. It is the extension of the established higher education sector to accommodate these institutions that has finally initiated a full-blown debate on mass higher education in Britain, since the 1992 legislation marked a point at which the age participation index of students in higher education had more than quadrupled since the mid-1960s, from 8 per cent to 28 per cent (Scott, 1995, p. 22). The debate continues because the sector is not unified. Scott (1995, p. 26) notes that

> a distinction remains between the old universities, which are chartered bodies, and the new universities, which are Parliamentary institutions established by Secretaries of State. This distinction is reflected

in contrasting patterns of governance and, less tangibly but more eloquently, in different institutional cultures, collegial or managerial.

It is in part through their belated, faint and rather incoherent protests at the introduction of managerial institutional cultures that the older universities have sought, unsuccessfully, to express their opposition to mass access to higher education. But changes in the structure of funding of universities during the 1980s, including continuing reductions in the unit of funding, as well as increases in the scale of higher educational provision, have necessitated the rapid introduction of new managerial and accounting techniques throughout the sector as a condition of survival. The new, post-polytechnic universities of the unified system are not only marked by their managerial institutional cultures; they are the major sources of provision of post-secondary education in management and are thus in a reflexive academic relation with their institutional cultures.

There is, finally, a fifth idea of the modern university – in many respects a more analytical phenomenon than the substantive institutional forms taken by the preceding four ideas. These are the various forms of open-access university, of which the Open University is clearly the most substantial. Indeed, it was established as a further stage of the post-Robbins expansion of the sector, at the beginning of the 1970s, and might arguably be grouped with them. But a mark of its success is the attempted extensions of provision that have been modelled on it. Among the more significant of these have been the University of the Third Age, for senior citizens, and the University of the Highlands and Islands, for small and physically disparate populations. Other attempts at emulation have a more rhetorical air: the Labour Party's University for Industry, for example:

> the Nineties equivalent of the Open University – will use satellite, cable. and the new information highways to give every home and workplace access to information, to skills and to teaching, to achieve . . . permanent educational opportunity for all. Switching on your computer for opportunities should be as natural as switching on your TV to watch a football match.
>
> (Blair, 1996, p. 33)

This idea of an open-access University for Industry follows in some senses from universities which are already established to provide specific vocational training for particular industries. McDonald's has a global Hamburger University, with national locations, at which all levels of staff are trained. The Disney Institute offers some sixty adult educational courses in what George Ritzer (1996) has described as 'the Disney fashion of infotainment'. The first 'on-line' universities have begun to emerge in North America, where the provision of continuing higher education through an established system of credit transfer between institutions with compatible unitized courses and modularized degree structures is already well established.

There are variations on and overlaps between these five broad ideas and their accompanying ideals – the private University of Buckingham, for example, which gained its charter during the 1980s, after the emergence of the post-Robbins universities and the binary system (but before the 1992 legislation designed to produce a unified system). Buckingham, which remains the only privately funded university in Britain, has pioneered a number of developments which, if current central government rhetoric is to be transformed into policy, could soon become routine structural features of higher education. It offers two-year degrees, with a fourth teaching term over the period of the summer vacation and a specialized infrastructure of provision related almost entirely to the incorporation of professional qualifications into its degrees. Indeed, a fuller morphology of the university system in Britain has been set out by Scott (1995, pp. 44–50) who identifies 12 subsectors which comprise the expanded universities sector and points out that the complete higher education system comprises at least 17 subsectors and subgroups to which 'must be added a further three to complete the post-compulsory education and training system' (Scott, 1995, p. 50).

## Functions of the modern university

It is scarcely surprising that a coherent view of the university is not to be found among this plethora of types of institution. The sheer variety of forms suggests that they are a response to frequently changing circumstances – an impression endorsed by the fact that most of the institutions have been established since the 1960s. Yet the character of the debate on contemporary British higher education is one of the problematics of the change from a traditional, selective, even meritocratically élitist system to one of mass provision, a change which, Scott (1995, p. 90) notes, 'coincides intriguingly' with a 'profound transformation of western, now world, society and of advanced economies'. I consider this a disingenuous contention, however, precisely because of the relatively recent differentiation of the higher education system into its diversity of forms: their emergence parallels closely enough the structural changes in the contemporary British socio-economic order to warrant enquiry into the reflexive causal relations between these two types of phenomenon.

It is possible to identify three clear functions that contemporary institutions of higher education can perform for modern society. First, they are *institutions of cultural reproduction*, in at least three senses: they can safeguard, by sustaining the continuity of cultural tradition, as Leavis proposes the university should; this may be tied to the related reproduction of a stratified social structure, such as Eliot insists is a necessary condition of high culture; and they provide an environment in which epistemological culture can be challenged, revised and renewed through exploration and innovation. This is related to the second function of the institutions of higher education, that of *research*: the institutions exist to provide for the pursuit of pure epistemological research, to explore the implications for society of the results of research, and are expected to advise on how those results might be translated into and implemented as policy. This relates, in turn, to the third function of higher education, that of *training*. Institutions of higher education are increasingly expected, as conditions of their funding, to adapt their provision to the changing occupational requirements of late industrial economies. The changing conditions and characteristics of these economies may themselves be a consequence of the epistemological research and innovations produced by universities and other institutions, which must train what has been termed a 'career-resilient workforce' (Waterman *et al.*, 1994) in the necessary transferable skills to sustain employment and/or survive unemployment.

These functions are the key to the reflexively causal relations between the proliferation of subsectors and subgroups of higher education institutions and changes in the structure and processes of contemporary society. They are the functions of institutions implicated in the volatile socio-cultural conditions of the 'post-'s: postmodern society, poststructuralist epistemology and postindustrial economy.

In the face of these changes, the least effectively performed of the functions of higher education is that of sustaining cultural continuity. This is inevitable if, as the conditions of the 'post-'s propose, modern society is in the process of a radical rupture with its past. But it is difficult to understand if the move towards mass provision is seen, erroneously, as in part a *cause* of the inability of the university to sustain continuity. This error is not only committed by conservative thinkers such as Eliot and Leavis. A more problematic and more current form is found in the faintly self-indulgent piety of cultural critics who include themselves in a superficial version of the vivid present on the grounds that:

> [i]f postmodernism means . . . the opening up to critical discourse of lines of enquiry which were formerly prohibited, of evidence which was previously inadmissible so that new and different questions can be asked and new and other voices can begin asking them; if it means the opening up of institutional and discursive spaces within which more fluid and plural social and sexual identities may develop; if it means the erosion of triangular formations of power and knowledge with the expert at the apex and the 'masses' at the base, if, in a word, it enhances our collective (and democratic) sense of possibility, then I for one am a postmodernist.
>
> (Hebdige, 1988, p. 226)

This neo-Kiplingesque paean to virtual social and cultural (un)reality implies a recipe for institutional dissolution that bears no recognizable relation to the institutional dilemmas of contemporary higher education. It assumes, on the basis of extensive descriptions of the (often abstract) theorizations of the 'post-'s, that the speculations concerning possible changes have actually been established in substantive institutional forms. The changes which have occurred in higher education, as in most other institutions, however, have tended to take the form of a redefinition of, rather than a revolution in, functions.

## Redefinition of functions

There are four distinct features of this redefinition. First, a change in the structure and rhetoric of state (central government) planning in contemporary British society, which has had significant consequences for higher education. Though the rhetoric is of a reduction in the role of the state, the practice has been to sustain the powers of the state, deploying them in the imposition of privatization of publicly owned and administered services, and of market funding structures on public expenditure – especially the institutions of local government, the welfare state and education. Most of the central government decisions which have affected the structure and funding of institutions of higher education, however, have been made on grounds which are either peripheral or extrinsic, and in many cases antithetical to their traditional concerns and organization. As well as the imposition of market funding principles, the expansion of access has been used to restructure the relation between employment and unemployment for the post-secondary and post-further-education cohort. The expansion of opportunities for taught postgraduate study has had comparable consequences for the graduate employment market. In both cases, the financial cost of these increased opportunities has had to be funded by student loans in addition to or instead of grants. Yet no policies have been developed to provide students with alternative funding opportunities in the ways, for example, that are well established in North America and being introduced in Australia, by providing jobs in the operation of universities themselves to enable students to work their way through their studies. This involves franchising of university services, with requirements on franchisees to use student labour, part-time employment of students in university clerical administration, as well as restructuring timetables on to blocked days to leave students free days on which they can work, and the introduction of summer terms and semesters. It represents the kind of thinking-through of the full implications of structural changes in funding that follows only when the changes are acknowledged consciously and implemented as changes in policy.

A second feature of the redefinition of functions of higher education that follows from the introduction of a market system to its structure of funding and provision has been the introduction of structures of accountability and an associated culture of fiscal and managerial audit. This has replaced traditional funding provisions of central and local government funding with systems of budgeting based upon contractual provision of training and/or research which are evaluated regularly in terms of the effectiveness of institutional performance. Auditing the adequacy of higher educational provision (what the Higher Education Funding Council for

England terms its fitness for purpose), endorses reductively the redefinition of students as consumers of teaching/learning, but with the virtual benefits implied by Hebdige of the capacious conceptual, sociological and political opportunities offered by postmodernism. These involve the superseding of traditional epistemological structures by expert and abstract systems which interact with actual environments to construct and reconstruct values and institutions which have been freed from the fixities and givens of traditional sociocultural orders and their associated 'social and sexual identities'. Scott (1995, p. 113) summarizes the process as a switch of emphasis

> from upward social mobility for a meritocratic élite to the development of a 'college culture' for the majority – from life chances to lifestyles, mirroring the larger shift towards post-industrialism. To some extent, and in the short term, class-based hierarchies harden as mobility slows. The decline of graduate careers reflects this change. But, in another sense, class society itself begins to dissolve as the links loosen between socio-cultural status and occupational categories (which themselves are becoming more volatile).

Thus the transformation of the sociological base and academic culture of higher education is central to the processes of modernization in the late twentieth-century world – if, that is, we accept that the logic of those processes is contained within the logic of the 'post-'s, the logic of a breach with, rather than a continuity of, tradition.

One challenge to this position, on the grounds that it will not provide the transferable skills required or subvert the rigidities of hierarchical social stratification, is formulated (by Phillips, 1996) as the more fundamental question of the value of the expansion of higher education. Increased provision of degrees, it is argued, simply masks deficiencies in more important occupational requirements for training in essential crafts and skills which can only be obtained through the experience of work itself. According to Phillips, the new, less differentiated social status that Scott suggests is now conferred by a degree, replaces the necessary technical skills for work, even in a post-industrial economy, with abstract (no doubt poststructuralist) theorizing in the pursuit of non-specific – and hence worthless – professionalization.

Phillips argues, ironically, that the reasons for this are endemic to British employers' competitive approach to occupational training – they do not want to train young people well enough to be of value to other employers – compounded by the reluctance of central government to take a strong directive approach to its occupational requirements. The implications of this view are that, in contrast to Scott's suggestion that higher education is central to modernization, as far as those responsible for contemporary *British* social, political, economic and cultural policies are concerned, it appears to be anything but a *key* feature. It is important to emphasize that this applies to contemporary Britain because of the effective vacuum in higher education policy over the past two decades, despite the changes in funding and the abolition of the binary distinction.

The most important indication of the vacuum has been a third feature of the redefinition of function in higher education, and one not sought, but not prevented effectively by the institutions themselves: the inability to prioritize the funding of pure research, either directly by the institutions themselves or by the funding councils. The latter have chosen to represent government practices to the institutions as their own policies for the encouragement of research – which they have variously termed applied, thematic or policy-related – rather than to represent the research interests and needs of the universities to government. This has benefited significantly the individual careers of some research council members, but has exacerbated the problems that stem from a lack of funds for pure research.

The fourth feature of redefinition of functions in higher education, which is also in part a consequence of the shift to market funding models, is the development of quite different patterns of academic provision. Increasingly, these are models which are designed to offer training rather than the more traditional, discursive senses of higher education, which are intended to enable institutions to compete with one another in offering both home and overseas students the transferable skills which they require in the post-Fordist labour market of the postindustrial economy. Students are thereby themselves redefined as consumers for the range of skills on offer. The structure of the postindustrial economy is characterized by an accelerating shift from material product manufacturing to provision of services concerned with increasingly rapid delivery of symbolic goods. What product manufacture does remain is transformed through processes of customization, and the occupational organization of both manufacturing and services is radically altered through the introduction, in a context of globalization, of practices of outsourcing of raw materials and production, and downsizing of firms and bureaucracies. Traditional occupational work, in the form of an organizational career, begins to be replaced by job 'portfolios' in which changing and adaptive (transferable) skills based on local and transient knowledge are temporarily contracted to the performance of short-term tasks. It is to these changing configurations in the division of labour of the postindustrial economy that the modern university seeks to adapt.

It is not entirely facetious to suggest that doing so would appear to risk producing graduates imbued with the epistemology of the 'post-'s, and with negative occupational competences and capacities. They risk being trained specifically for what André Gorz (1982; 1985) once identified, in a proto-postmodern trope, as the leisure society – the society of non-work, in which the overwhelming majority of human occupational tasks had been taken over by machines. The qualities that can be expected of the graduates of the mass-access higher education institutions of the twenty-first century are those that will equip them, during the lifetime of non-employment and lack of occupation (in the traditional sense) which would appear to await them, to construct and reconstruct their identities in terms of the myriad of non-traditional features of lifestyles which will be available to them instead of the traditional and outdated life chances. This may prove to be exceptionally hard work, far more exhausting than the indignity of manual labour, the monotony of clerical skill, the stress injuries of repetitive keyboard manipulation or the exhaustion of exercising professional judgement. The importance of this work is the key to how difficult it may be, for it involves sustaining the ultimate illusion of postmodernists – that virtual realities have become actualized. In order to sustain such an illusion, the graduates of the new millennium may have to be completely absorbed by the commoditization of images and ideas and dedicated to pursuing the realization of their lifestyles by consuming them – thus elevating the injunction 'shop until you drop' to an ontic vocation! The logic of the 'post-'s is one which informs speculative theorizing, but is not yet a socio-logic; nor, therefore, does it have substantive social or cultural institutional correlates, and so cannot provide for an adequate consideration of the social role of higher education.

## Disinterestedness and the modern university

The modern university is deeply implicated in the processes of social and cultural change. Yet most ideas of the modern university require that it should reflect upon the conditions and consequences of these processes as well as participate in their initiation, implementation and consolidation. Institutions of higher education cannot disengage from such practices, nor is it desirable that they should, since it is only through engagement with them that they can sustain their relevance for modern society. But nor is it desirable that institutions of higher education should transform themselves, or allow themselves to be transformed, into either instrumental agencies for training potential employees in transferable skills or environments for the exploration of alternative lifestyles for virtual sociocultural realities.

Rather than being subjected to such reductive roles, institutions of higher education constitute the environments and provide the expertise and qualities required to reflect critically on contemporary social processes. Without such critical reflection we cannot expect either to plan social changes, or to respond to their unforeseen and/or unintended consequences intelligently, rationally and humanely. This requires, therefore, a clear sense of the place and role of the institutions of higher education in contemporary, late modern society – a sense which depends upon the ability of institutions of higher education to develop disinterested provision for education, training and research. By way of a conclusion that will provide a basis for further discussion, therefore, I want to suggest three features of this role, all of which provide for the detachment of institutions of higher education from automatic reduction to conditions of instrumental functionality:

1. The role of higher education is to promote disinterested research for its own sake. It is far from clear that this can be achieved or sustained under an imposed structure of market funding.

2. The social and cultural responsibility of higher education is to take a critical stance in relation to collective, societal politics, purposes and plans. The conduct of disinterested research is vital to this.
3. The university is committed to providing the most effective conditions for the pursuit of epistemological excellence by the most able from among the community which it serves. Entry to the university must therefore be disinterestedly selective of its students and selection must be based upon merit demonstrated by achievement.

This implies a redifferentiation of the British higher education system into a system of plural provision which the attempt to produce a unified system appears to disguise, yet actually reinforces without reflection. The basis for this would appear already to be available by the differentiation that the senior universities have made already between those who are members of the Russell and/or the 94 groups and the remainder of the so-called old universities. Both groups differentiate themselves from the so-called new universities and other institutions of higher education. There might be an institutional basis for this via provision for a differentiated basis for funding for three categories of university: those that are primarily concerned with large-scale funded projects in pure and applied research and postgraduate teaching; those that sustain a balance between smaller-scale and individual funded research, undergraduate and postgraduate teaching; and those that are concerned primarily with undergraduate teaching combined with some professional and vocational postgraduate training. One effect – perhaps unintended – of such restructuring may be to open the full debate which is required on the consequences for both research and vocational training of unplanned expansion into a mass higher education system.

# Part 2

The University in Society

# 6

# Intellectuals: Inside and Outside the University

*Russell Jacoby*

## Binary categories

Current academic wisdom would have an easy time with the subject of intellectuals 'inside and outside' the university. For this wisdom recoils before binary opposition. It would instruct us that 'inside' and 'outside' smack of Eurocentrism, if not Western colonialism; it would teach us that all binary categories bespeak domination, and all must be 'problematized'. These reflections would make way for a discussion of 'outsiders' and 'marginality' and 'boundaries' as terms that must be endlessly 'contextualized', since they lack fixed meanings. The issue of intellectuals 'inside' and 'outside' would become a different project.

I must confess my ignorance: I have never understood the rote critique of binary categories or what drives it. It may originate in some primitive conception of Hegel's dialectic as moving between and beyond thesis and antithesis. Whatever its source, not the least of its problems is that the critique of binarism is cranked out on computers constructed out of binary switches, routines and numbers. A recent history of mathematics that covers computers includes an appreciation of the 'binary assumption' (McLeish, 1991, p. 227). Yet this binarism does not seem to bother the critics of binarism; at least they never mention it. To put this another way: the critique of binarism is sustained by binarism.

Of course, the conventional criticism is not all wrong: outside and inside are hardly absolute categories. They are shot through with history and are far from fixed. Moreover, they are both objective and subjective categories with economic and psychological dimensions. Evidently precision is not possible. Yet these configurations do not end analysis; they only mean we should be vigilant – perhaps particularly vigilant about easy talk that nothing exists outside of texts and shifting social definitions. To cite from a typical postmodernist article that deals with science: 'A simple criterion for science to qualify as postmodern is that it be free from any dependence on the concept of objective truth'. After quoting Derrida on Einstein, the author gives an example:

> The key point is that . . . any space-time point, if it exists at all, can be transformed into any other. In this way the infinite-dimensional invariance group erodes the distinction between observer and observed; the $\pi$ of Euclid and the $G$ of Newton, formerly thought to be constant and universal, are now perceived in their ineluctable historicity; and the putative observer becomes fatally de-centered . . .
>
> (Sokal, 1996a, p. 226, 218)[1]

This is standard postmodern stuff that recently appeared in a leading journal, *Social Text*, published by Duke University Press. Unknown to its editors, it was a parody written by a New York University physicist. The editors – until the author publicly revealed his little joke – saw nothing alarming in the article; on the contrary, they liked and published it. The piece seemed little different from many they printed.[2] The problem becomes that all of reality is subjectivized, just turf for contending interpretations.

If anything can be decentred or problematized, then 'inside' and 'outside' are simply constructs, lacking reality. To shift terms a bit, with no centre anything might be the margins. One of Derrida's collections is titled *Margins of Philosophy*; he 'seeks to blur the line which separates a text from its controlled margin'. Derrida (1986, p. xxiii) wants 'to reckon with the entire logic of the margin . . . to recall that beyond the philosophical text there is not a blank, virgin, empty margin, but another text, a weave of difference forces without any present center'.

With just decentred texts, who can say what is outside or inside? Evidently anyone can and does. The problem is this: the terms and categories begin to lose their meaning. 'Outside' is whatever and whoever feels outside. Leftist academics in particular, no matter how esteemed and established, often claim to see themselves or feel themselves as outsiders. For instance, Gaytri Spivak, a chaired professor at Columbia University, a translator of Derrida, and a much lionized speaker at academic conferences, perceives herself as 'marginalized'. With no irony she writes of the 'explosion of marginality studies' in American universities and her role in it. Moreover, she is not only part of the marginality industry, she has been marginalized by the 'deconstructive establishment' (Spivak, 1993, p. ix).

On occasion the irony or at least the difficulty of successful marginality strikes her. She quotes the description of a literary project that crossed her desk: 'Taking the "magical realism" of García Márquez as a paradigmatic case of Third World literary production, I will argue that science fiction . . . may be considered, so to speak, the Third World fiction of the industrialized nations . . .'. She asks: 'How is the claim to marginality being negotiated here? The radicals of the industrialized nation want to be the Third World.' Yet she gets only half of it. Spivak is quoting 'from a grant proposal written by a brilliant young Marxist academic'. That marginal, would-be Third World

Marxist intellectuals are filling out grant applications provokes no comment (Spivak, 1993, p. 57).

## Insiders who pretend to be outsiders

Perhaps I can put what has happened in recent decades this way: once intellectuals were outsiders who wanted to be insiders. Now they are insiders who pretend to be outsiders – a claim that can be sustained only by subjectivizing marginality. This is not the whole story, but may be half of it. The other half is the admission, even celebration, of the new inside status as career professionals. These are not opposite events; rather they form two sides of the same process. Both signify the overcoming of older reality, which to be sure was always partly mythic, of the independent intellectual.

Most commentators have welcomed the demise of the independent intellectual. It is well to remember that this 'rootless' or 'free-floating' individual was an anathema to the right – but also to the left. To most Marxists, intellectuals were at best lackeys of the bourgeoisie, at worst anarchistic or unreliable. Marxists regularly denounced intellectuals as 'waverers', distant from real life and its political battles (cf. Bering, 1978).

Endless references to Gramsci and his ideas on hegemony, a favourite for cultural and postmodern theorists, do not change the fact that his ideas on intellectuals did not especially diverge from those of other Marxists; he also wanted to root intellectuals in material and industrial life. 'The mode of being of the new intellectual', he stated, 'can no longer consist of eloquence ... but in active participation in practical life, as constructor, organizer, "permanent persuader"' (Gramsci, 1971, p. 10).

For similar reasons conservative and reactionary thinkers also denounced the free-floating intellectuals, whom they considered out of touch with real life. Maurice Barrès, the anti-Dreyfusard, called intellectuals 'logicians of the absolute'. He considered them 'deracinated' internationalists who trade in abstractions like 'Justice' and 'Truth' and 'who no longer spontaneously feel any rapport' with the nation. From here it less than a half-step to anti-Semitism: the Jews are deracinated people who have no commitment to the nation. 'For us,' stated Barrès, 'the nation is our soil and our ancestors; it is the land of our dead.' For the Jewish intellectuals, on the other hand, nationalism is an 'idea' or a 'prejudice to destroy' (Barrès, 1925, pp. 59, 49, 68).

For all his faults, Mannheim sought to systematize the place of intellectuals as permanent outsiders, a group that had no fixed roots. 'We want to find a home, a world,' he wrote in 1921, 'because we feel that we have no place in this world' (cited in Hoeges, 1994, p. 229). For his troubles he earned the wrath of both left and right. To Karl August Wittfogel, writing in a communist newspaper in 1931, Mannheim's ideas on 'the relatively "unattached intellectuals"' smack of crude 'bourgeois apologetics'. 'It is plain that the bourgeois intellectual can only be fully useful to his class if he can "prove" by some means that he basically stands above the class, that his views are not those of the ruling, exploiting class' (Wittfogel, 1990, p. 234). To Han Speier, writing in a socialist journal, '[t]he intelligentsia will no longer know the "homelessness of the spirit" (Mannheim) once it realizes that its co-operation is valuable to the Party' (Speier, 1990, p. 220). For a conservative like Ernst Robert Curtius, Mannheim's ideas express a 'variant of European nihilism . . . a state of mind, already well described by Nietzsche, of uprooted, modern intellectual strata' (Curtius, 1990, p. 114).

While Mannheim inspired much writing about the sociology of knowledge and sociological relativism, few followed his analysis of intellectuals as 'un-attached' and 'between classes' (Mannheim, 1985, pp. 157–8). To be sure, discussion of intellectuals has persisted, and in recent years has flourished. Why? Two reasons can be hazarded – political and sociological. Mannheim saw himself as working out some consequences of Marxism in a period of crisis and uncertainty. He quoted the famous line of Max Weber: 'The materialistic conception of history is not to be compared to a cab that one can enter or alight from at will, for once they enter it, even the revolution-aries themselves are not free to leave it' (cited in Mannheim, 1985, p. 67).

For many intellectuals, the Marxist cab provided a theory of their place and role. One could cite Lenin or Lukács or Gramsci with confidence of participating in an ongoing project that addressed intellectuals. No more. Today the cab has stalled or stopped, and all are alighting, wondering where or what the next move is. In other words, the collapse of communism in recent years has forced intellectuals to re-examine themselves and their roles. Where Mannheim saw himself as carrying out the logic of Marxism, today the logic has lost conviction.

## Institutionalized intellectuals

The structural shifts that affect intellectuals have in recent decades become so obvious that few can deny them. If Mannheim's analysis of the independ-ent intellectuals seemed questionable for the late 1920s, it is downright impossible for the late 1990s. Intellectuals seem increasingly 'attached' or affiliated or institutionalized. In this perspective, Mannheim can be seen as the last theorist of the independent intellectuals, not the first. After Mannheim, the classic vision of intellectuals as independent and rootless makes way for a view of intellectuals as dependent and anchored.

In recent decades – to generalize crudely – we have regular studies of intellectuals as new professionalized groupings, part and parcel of society. For instance, a new book concludes by noting that intellectuals have moved 'from the margins of society towards a more central position'. 'Those insti-tutions and processes which traditionally have been formative for intellectuals – the university, the literary and political public sphere . . . – have in late modern societies become more and more institutionalized, professionalized and commercialized' (Eyerman, 1994, pp. 190–1). At best, we have theories that intellectuals themselves, by virtue of their numbers and qualities, form a 'new class'. No one can argue any longer that intellectuals form a independent group outside the major institutions.

Of course, cultural life does not neatly follow political and social shifts. What might be called the classic argument about intellectuals – marginalized dissenters who attack injustice – has not disappeared. It runs from Voltaire to Said. The 'men of letters', wrote Voltaire, are 'isolated writers', who have neither 'arguified on the benches of the universities nor said things by halves in the academies; and these have nearly all been persecuted'. He adds that if you write odes to the monarch, 'you will be well received. Enlighten men, and you will be crushed' (Voltaire, 1972, p. 274).

A virtually straight line can be drawn from Voltaire to Said, whose recent *Representations of the Intellectual* advances an idea of the intellectual as a marginalized and vulnerable critic. The intellectual, he writes, is 'someone whose place it is publicly to raise embarrassing questions, to confront orthodoxy and dogma . . . to be someone who cannot easily be co-opted by governments or corporations' (Said, 1994, p. 32). The intellectual, he states, 'always has a choice either to side with the weaker, the less well represented, the forgotten or ignored, or to side with the more powerful' (Said, 1994, p. 1).

> And there is something fundamentally unsettling about intellectuals who have neither offices to protect nor territory to consolidate and guard; self-irony is therefore more frequent than pomposity, directness more than hemming and hawing. But there is no dodging the inescapable reality that such representations by intellectuals will neither make them friends in high places nor win them official honors. It is a lonely condition . . .
>
> (Said, 1994, p. xviii).

This is a touching portrait, but what relationship does it bear to reality? No 'hemming and hawing'? No offices or territory to defend? Lonely existence. Where? Maybe in Algeria, but hardly in the United States or France. Can we say that Derrida, for instance, or Said himself, lead unrecognized marginalized lives? (And, if anything, Derrida has raised 'hemming and hawing' to a science.) It would be more accurate to state the opposite: they and other oppositional intellectuals hold distinguished positions at major institutions; that they are regularly wined and dined, and receive not only generous salaries but also handsome payments for their occasional lectures. These souls are very much part of the establishment.

Many of these individuals, like Cornel West or Camille Paglia, cannot be contacted directly, but operate with agents, who deal with their fees and schedules. Of course, these intellectuals often announce their marginality, but their marginality seems more and more, as it were, marginal. bell hooks – the lower case is part of her *nomme de guerre* – a distinguished professor at City College New York and a leading black feminist, recently recounted grievous tales of marginality; for instance, on an aeroplane journey the good professor was outraged because a black friend with a coach-class ticket could not join her in first class, since the adjacent seat was already taken by a white passenger – an incident of such proportions that it inspired her *Killing Rage*.

Are these tales of marginality or privilege? Or she recounts other shocking stories of victimization; for instance, a black Harvard graduate student reported that in a class on feminist theory Professor hooks's own work was read. 'Yet the day it was discussed in class the white woman professor declared that no one was really moved by my work . . . this young black woman felt both silenced and victimized' (hooks, 1995, pp. 8–10, 60–1). Marginality gets defined or redefined on the basis of comments about a book in a Harvard graduate seminar.

The point is: any sober appraisal of intellectuals in North America and Europe must not simply second or celebrate the classic picture of the vulnerable and independent critic, but consider a newer and divergent reality. Any analysis must to entertain the possibility that marginality is less a reality than a pose and that the self-defined outsiders are actually consummate insiders. Indeed, Aijaz Ahmad (1992) has recently suggested that the new discipline of 'postcolonial literature', which focuses exclusively on marginalized literature, is less a subversive field than a good career move for largely upper-class Asian immigrants searching for jobs in metropolitan universities.

To be sure, and one must be careful here, the link between institutional success and intellectual contribution is not direct. On the contrary. Or, to alter the terms, one might be an institutional insider and an intellectual outsider. Fat salaries and secure positions hardly preclude original and subversive work; nor do paltry wages and insecure positions guarantee revolutionary and critical thought. This cannot be stated forcefully enough. Yet this is true on the individual, not the general level; here sociological observations are valid and necessary efforts to assess the long-range shifts and their general consequences for intellectual life.

## Tenured radicals?

Oddly, of late, it is the conservatives who have become the Marxist materialists – at least *vis-à-vis* the radical professors; they charge that current intellectuals are 'tenured radicals' who mouth leftist platitudes while living off government largess. In the face of such critiques, the leftists have retreated to utter idealism; they see themselves as cutting-edge intellectuals risking life and limb challenging bourgeois hegemony. They fail to mention their earnings or employer, the state or major institutions.

Institutionalization, professionalization and the fall of communism have exacted a toll. In recent years, numerous discussions have taken place, mainly in Germany, France and the United States, about the new situation of intellectuals. Often these discussions have been framed by the question, where are the intellectuals? Where are our Jean-Paul Sartres or Heinrich Bölls or Lewis Mumfords? As the German novelist Bodo Kirchhoff states (cited in Vogt, 1993):

> In Germany there once was a time, when writers had power over public opinion. That era is over. The collapse of socialism has driven the last remaining old-style authors – idealists, utopians, martyrs, court jesters, renegades, the unclassifiable – out of the paradise of friend/enemy dichotomies . . . We are all colleagues in impotence.

Of course, this sentiment is not universally shared. What is amazing, however, is how much is agreed upon: that intellectuals have become professionals and professors – insiders. Surprisingly for many liberals and leftists this marks an advance.

Let me use as a jumping-off point Tony Judt's book on French intellectuals, *Past Imperfect: French Intellectuals 1944–1956* – a book which has some serious shortcomings. Judt's book is an upbeat report of the decline of French public intellectuals of the recent past – the Sartres and Merleau-Pontys. He labels them 'intellectuals-as-heroes' who suffered from serious contradictions, flaws, frauds and blindness. He recounts a happy story of their decline and replacement by new academics and professionals, who are much more responsible and careful thinkers. Let me quote him:

> Although there are still today some prominent intellectuals whose renown and income derive largely from their journalism and books, the rise of the social sciences and the expansion of the tertiary sector in education have given professors a new lease on life. Thus they enter the intellectual arena as experts . . . This encourages a degree of modesty and care, deriving from the typical professorial sense it is one's colleagues rather than the world whom one has to convince . . . This marks a distinct change from earlier decades, when the writings of Malraux, Camus, Sartre, Mounier, and their peers, often half-informed, frequently lazy and ignorant, provoked no such rebukes . . . In the civil society of today's intellectual community, the market operates with reasonable efficiency . . . Left to their own devices, intellectuals are thus better placed to retain their local influence if they can point to the imprimatur of quality that comes with institutional attachment and disciplinary conventions. The correspondence between the decline of the great public intellectuals and the resurrection of the professors is thus no mere coincidence.
>
> (Judt, 1992, pp. 296–7)

This analysis explicitly states that professionalization, the market, disciplinary conventions and institutional attachments are all excellent, improving the quality of intellectual life and discourse, which used to be rotten and corrupt. Putting aside Judt's cheap shots at the classic French intellectuals (cf. Wall, 1994), what is striking is not just the cheery and cheering analysis – intellectual life is getting better and better – but how much this position is shared, with different twists, across the political spectrum. Feminists, poststructuralists, deconstructionists, postcolonialists, and so on, celebrate the demise of the old intellectuals and cheer the rise of new types of intellectuals and new types of publics; like Judt, they are more or less championing themselves and their own publics.

Jean-François Lyotard, who probably does not usually agree with Judt, offers a position that is similar. In his *Tombeau de l'Intellectuel* he tells us that the old-style intellectual depended on the appeal of a 'universal subject'. However, professionalization and the modern theoretical physics have upset the idea of a universal subject. Intellectuals can no longer intervene in public affairs in the name of a universal public; the only possibilities are 'local' and 'defensive'. For Lyotard these developments are less 'pessimistic' than 'optimistic': 'The decline, perhaps collapse, of the universal idea might free thought and life of obsession with totality' (Lyotard, 1984b, pp. 11–12).

Like Judt, Jonathan Culler, an English professor, offers a happy tale of professionalization; he protests against 'the crisis narratives' that blame professionalization and academization. He stoutly maintains that 'we must assert the value not just of specialization but of professionalization also, explaining how professionalization makes thought possible'. Culler turns misty-eyed on the virtues of specialization; it gives rise to 'serious' 'works of criticism or scholarship', not to be confused with 'newspaper articles', 'works of popularization' or 'especially commentary'. It leads to the judicious and democratic judgments by peers.

> While reducing capriciousness and favoritism in important decisions, this progress in professionalism shifts power from the vertical hierarchy of the institutions that employs a critic to a horizontal system of evaluation. Critical writing, which is the medium of exchange of this system, thus becomes central to the professional situation and identity of teachers of literature.
>
> (Culler, 1988, pp. 55, 30)

Even so cautious and careful thinker as Michael Walzer joins in. In *The Company of Critics* Walzer argues that contemporary critics are not in any real sense 'alienated' from their societies. In fact they are often well-renumerated full professors. Contemporary social critics 'are not peculiarly hostile to the societies in which they live; they are not peculiarly alienated from those societies'. And they write what Walzer (1988, pp. 8–11) applauds as 'mainstream criticism'. With some verve, in *Interpretation and Social Criticism* he criticizes the conventional picture of the intellectual critic as an alienated outsider as bad for criticism. Marginality is not 'a condition that makes for disinterest, dispassion, open-mindedness, or objectivity'. 'Disconnected criticism' tends towards 'manipulation and compulsion'. Walzer, a lifetime member of a research institute, the Institute for Advanced Studies, which gathers for weekly lunches, offers a different and better 'model' for the intellectual: someone who is member of the learned club, 'the local judge, the connected critic, who earns his authority, or fails to do so, by arguing with his fellows' (Walzer, 1987, pp. 37, 39).

Finally, consider Andrew Ross's comments in *No Respect: Intellectuals and Popular Culture.* He writes that today it is 'clear' that the 'mantle of opposition no longer rests upon the shoulders of an autonomous avant-garde: neither the élite metropolitan intellectuals . . . nor the romantic neo-bohemians'. If there is any role – and there might not be – it is with Foucauldian 'technical' or 'specific' intellectuals; and with 'professional humanists' who play a 'specialist influence' in 'an important area of contestation within the academy'. This has enormously opened up the curriculum to marginal groups. Ross states that 'the achievements of this new specialism have run up against the same reactionary consensus of left and right, each unswervingly loyal to their respective narratives of decline' (Ross, 1989, pp. 210–11).

# The obsolescence of the old-style intellectual

It seems to me that these positions fairly well cover the political and theoretical spectrum. With various amounts of enthusiasm they celebrate the obsolescence of the old-style intellectual, presumably universalist in claim, who addressed a universal public; with various amounts of pleasure they announce the new specialist intellectual, university-based, who is plugged into professional networks and specialist audiences; and with various amounts of disdain they reject 'narratives' of decline and decay and see progress in intellectual life.

A large part of these facts cannot be disputed; much of the interpretation can be. For starters, the easy references to the 'narratives' of decline and crisis appeal to a counter-narrative of progress and advance, a 'narrative' which seems as dubious as that of decline. Has there been such obvious 'progress' and 'advances' in intellectual life? Are the new literary critics, like Ross himself or Stanley Fish, so obviously better than earlier ones like Edmund Wilson? Are new French intellectuals like Bourdieu so clearly superior to earlier ones like Henri Lefebvre? Moreover, for those who like to see themselves at the cutting edge, nothing is more conventional that the notion of relentless progress.

The embrace, and often celebration, of professionalization is strange. The history and critique of professionalization is hardy new or unknown; on the contrary, it is common and accepted. Yet it coexists with an opposite, the promotion of specialized knowledge and a specialized audience. Obviously, in these matters, 'either/ors' are neither appropriate nor desirable. To be both a supporter of professionalization and a critic of its excesses or deformations is not inconsistent. Yet there is little doubt that the tide runs against non-professional and non-accredited thinkers and writers: they belong to suspect past of privilege and hierarchy.

At least in the United States, the embrace of professionalization has been nourished by turn-of-the-century progressivism and Marxism; left intellectuals have seen expert knowledge as part of a modernization which they generally applaud. Specialism signalled the advancement of science, and science for leftists was generally welcomed. Conversely, conservatives, more loyal to pre-industrial models, had more doubts about professionalization and professionalized knowledge. To jump to the present, it is more the conservatives who have remained committed to a model of the general intellectual, and leftists who have abandoned it as nostalgic, if not reactionary. Conservatives object to professionalization, and leftists applaud it.

## Conclusion: intellectuals and the public sphere

Let me close by taking up a topic which focuses on a kindred conceptual issue: the problem of the public sphere, which Habermas pushed into the centre of debate. To discuss intellectuals inside and outside the university entails discussing the nature of public spheres. Presumably, the classic independent intellectuals were sustained by a general reading public, itself the by-product of urbanization and education. Newer intellectuals address, if not smaller, then more fragmented, professionalized shifting publics.

Leftist critics see in the general public sphere what they see in the classic public intellectuals: at best, nostalgia for what never was; at worst, a sham and an apology for élitism. One collection that tackles the issue is aptly titled *The Phantom Public Sphere* (Robbins, 1993). With a certain amount of justice, critics hammer away at Habermas's concept as misleading. One criticism of Habermas's concept concludes that the public sphere 'was an arena of contested meanings, in which different and opposing publics manoeuvred for space and from which certain "publics" (women, subordinate nationalities, popular classes like the urban poor, the working class, and peasantry) have been excluded altogether' (Eley, 1992, pp. 325–6).

The problem with this criticism is not that it is flatly wrong. Rather, like the criticism of universalist intellectuals it ends by celebrating partial publics and mythologizing (or subjectivizing) rebellions. The critique of Habermas's idea of public sphere as static, masculine and exclusionary does not simply recognize marginal 'public spheres', but moves towards embracing them as better and more subversive. They are dubbed part of counterpublics or 'subaltern counterpublics' (Fraser, 1992, p. 123). From here it is a short step to interpreting any or all forms of response to cultural life as drenched with rebellion.

For instance, cultural studies experts argue that 'talk television' or 'consuming' constitute a new kind of public oppositional activity. 'Consumption', writes one critic of Habermas, 'sustains a counterpublicity that cuts against the self-contradictions of the bourgeois public sphere.' This author also argues that 'graffiti', mainly the work of a 'black male subculture', also makes up 'a kind of counterpublicity', and he quotes another interpretation of graffiti that views it as 'a critique of the status of all artistic artifacts, indeed a critique of all privatized consumption' (Warner, 1993, pp. 254–255).

The critique of the classic intellectual and the general public sphere is of one piece; it draws on the suspicion that universals are tools of manipulation and domination; that these abstractions are both false and tools of power. A larger philosophical issue, which is hardly discussable in a small compass, underlies these political beliefs.

To put it sharply, the suspicion of universals is suspicious. Local and specific concepts serve to defend local and specific institutions; historically abstractions have been progressive. Perhaps an intellectual footnote can be permitted here. In the 1960s Herbert Marcuse championed what he labeled 'the great refusal', a call to refuse co-operation with a murderous economic and social system. The 'great refusal' was an eminently political, perhaps anarchistic, idea. It derived, however, from a philosophical discussion by the English-American philosopher Alfred North Whitehead about the nature of universals. Whitehead noted that universals in art and criticism transcend their particular cases. This made the universal untrue in an exact sense. Any particular 'red' flower is less than the universal colour 'red'. Does that 'red' exist? Yes. How about equality? This is contradicted everywhere, perhaps even by those who uphold it. Does that make it untrue? In *Science and the Modern World* Whitehead (1964, p. 143) stated:

> The truth that some proposition respecting an actual occasion is untrue may express the vital truth as to the aesthetic achievement. It expresses the 'great refusal' which is its primary characteristic. An event is decisive in proportion to the importance (for it) of its untrue propositions . . . These transcendent entities have been termed 'universals'.

This 'great refusal' has often, not always, inhered in universal propositions about equality and rights. It sustains intellectuals of the recent and not so recent past who have spoken out. In a recent essay António Ribeiro (1995) reminds us of the role that Karl Krauss played at one point. In July 1927 Viennese citizens and workers gathered to protest against a court decision that acquitted several people accused of murdering a socialist and an eight-year-old boy. The crowd was fired upon by the police; scores were killed and hundreds wounded. Because of its inability to act, or even react, one historian has called 15 July 1927 'the first profound crisis of Austrian socialism in the interwar period' (Rabinbach, 1983, p. 33).[3]

Several months after the event, however, Karl Kraus put up a placard with a few brief lines. 'To the Police Chief of Vienna, Johann Schober: I ask you to resign. Karl Kraus, editor of the Fackel.' Kraus was acting as the classic universal intellectual, entering the public sphere to protest against misdeeds (Ribeiro, 1995). If that model – in its appeal to universal truths and its presentation of a universal intellectual – is old-fashioned, it is not obsolete.

# Notes

1. The first quotation is actually a citation from another work that Sokal uses.
2. This act of parody has already given rise to a vast number of commentaries, including by the author himself (Sokal, 1996b; 1996c).
3. For a personal account of the events of 15 July 1927, see Wilhelm Reich (1976, pp. 22–47).

# 7

# Universities and Public Policy

*William Melody*

... the wider social role of the university is now up for grabs. It is no longer clear what the place of the university is within society nor what the exact nature of that society is.

(Readings, 1996, p. 2).

Mechanisation ... has been responsible for monopolies in the field of knowledge; ... The conditions of freedom of thought are in danger of being destroyed by science, technology, and the mechanisation of knowledge ...

(Innis, 1951)[1]

## Introduction

Both the idea of the university, and the university institutions of the day, have been the subject of spirited debate periodically throughout the entire history of universities. The debate has been most vigorous when the universities of the time were under attack by the dominant institutions in society – church, state, or, in more recent times, business. Now is such a time in the UK, USA, Canada and other countries. An increasing volume of literature of all kinds (scholarly treatises, government reports, journal and magazine articles) is examining the role of the university in modern society. It is a subject of media coverage and even talk-back radio.

The current debate about the university is an issue far more central to both public policy and wider public discussion than any before it. Clearly universities have a vested interest in this debate as it directly affects their funding and the external influence of government and business on their research, teaching and other activities. The university ought to be well positioned to present a substantive and convincing case justifying its essential role in society, past, present and future. Yet in the market-place of ideas, the institution in society with the primary mission of generating and disseminating ideas has not been doing well, either in defending its existing role, or in providing compelling visions of its future role. Neither the theoretical explanations nor the substantive evidence being proffered have been found convincing by the rest of society. Ironically, in the transition to the future 'information society' and 'knowledge economy', the university is more generally seen as a part of the problem, not the solution.

Traditionally the university has seen itself to be detached from, and above, the fray of public policy debate. Periodic participation in public policy debate by university faculty members is generally regarded as 'service to the community', not professional accomplishment. It is something neither to be encouraged nor rewarded, although providing private advice to captains of industry and government has become a mark of distinction in some circles. As the university prepares itself for the information society of the future, there are several reasons why it must seriously reconsider its relation to, and participation in, public policy debate, not just on university policies, but as apart of a redefined educational mission. This requires a reconception of the idea, role and responsibilities of the university in the future.

This chapter examines some of the issues that bear on the possibility for university participation in public policy debate, not simply as a defensive reaction to external criticism and reduced government funding, but rather as a natural extension of the university's traditional concerns, that of fulfilling a role in society that is not being served well and that only the university can fulfil in twenty-first-century society. The university in this context is the large, diversified, multi-disciplinary, undergraduate and postgraduate, teaching and research institution that now dominates the higher education landscape in the USA, UK and Canada. I do not address the role of small colleges and other specialist institutions which, it is assumed, will continue to serve different roles in a pluralist educational system, although they too may need to reconsider their roles in an 'information society'.

## Beyond the idealist notion of the university

Graham Wallas (1934) and Harold Innis (1951), among others, have described how the oral tradition of Greek civilization provided the conditions most favourable to creative thought, and expressed concern that these favourable conditions were gradually disappearing. As Innis (1951, p. 191) states: 'The oral tradition is overwhelmingly significant when the subject-matter is human action and feeling, and it is important in the discovery of new truth but of very little value in disseminating it'. The decline of the oral tradition was attributed primarily to the 'quantitative pressure of modern knowledge' and 'the increasing mechanisation of knowledge' (ibid.). Improvements in science, and communication technologies in particular (ranging from writing, papyrus and the printing press, to radio), were seen as part of a shifting emphasis (or 'bias', as used by Innis) away from a focus on creative thought and discovery of new truth, and towards conservation and standardization of existing knowledge primarily for dissemination.

The assessments of Wallas and Innis were made before the massive post-war expansion of universities or the pervasive societal penetration of television, telephone and computing. These developments exacerbate the historic trends these authors documented far beyond anything they could have imagined. They provide an explanation why the primary function of the modern university is to disseminate institutionalized knowledge – that is, conventional wisdom. It still has a role for creative thought, but this is by now a relatively minor one that has been all but overwhelmed by its massively expanded dissemination role.

It is thus perhaps not surprising that when the university attempts to defend its current position in society, and the enormous resources it now absorbs, by resorting to the idealist notion of the university as a community of scholars which must be supported and protected from outside interference so that it may seek new truths through creative thought, it is treated with disbelief or disdain. The idealist notion may still have relevance to small colleges with large endowments which by their liberal arts traditions, financial independence, generally wealthy clientele and very smallness are able to exercise a greater freedom of choice in selecting their future role in society. But universities long ago outgrew the idealist conception. Most universities founded in the last century never had a possibility to consider it. Today the university is a large and important institution in society serving a number of public purposes, the most significant of which is knowledge dissemination. The idea of the university must be conceived around the reality that the university has become a major public institution in society and must be examined in that context.

## Institutional reform of the university

The funding of new universities over the last century, and the major expansion of many of the older ones, was not to expand curiosity-driven creative thought, but rather to serve what were seen as important public purposes. In the USA during the nineteenth century, public land-grant universities were established in many states for the primary purposes of providing 'an instrument of service throughout the state and a source of expert advice to its legislature' (Bok, 1982, p. 3). These have grown to become the massive state universities which now reflect the most prevalent conception of a modern US university, the activities of which have served as a model for many other universities, including some privately funded universities (Kerr, 1963).

This growth has been stimulated by a widespread belief that a university degree would provide both access to good employment opportunities and an increase in the productivity of the economy. This led to a rapid growth in student enrolments. Professional schools in medicine, law, business and other areas were well established to serve the needs of government, industry and the professions. In the USA, more than 50 per cent of high-school graduates now seek some kind of university-level education. Both government and industry began funding major special-purpose research programmes at the universities, mostly in science and technology, directed to support important objectives of those institutions. Beginning in the 1960s, these programmes were expanded to include social issues and were accompanied by a significant expansion in the social sciences.

This is a well-documented and widely understood transformation of both the idea and the role of the modern university in the United States. Derek Bok (1982, pp. 7–8), former president of Harvard, has noted:

> In these ways, as society came to rely more and more on universities, universities in turn grew ever more dependent on society for the money required to support their expanding activities . . . In short, by 1975, the federal government was beginning to move on many fronts to regulate academic policies in ways that would bring them into closer conformity with national needs.

Developments along a similar path have occurred in the UK and Canadian university communities. Although they started later, and they have neither grown quite as rapidly nor been as directly tied to implementing public policy objectives as the USA, they are moving rapidly along a similar path. The UK commitment to these goals can be traced at least back to the Robbins Report in the early 1960s (Committee on Higher Education, 1963), if not earlier.[2] UK university expansion grew roughly in parallel with, indeed if not as part of, the welfare state. A conception of most universities as public institutions, charged with providing services to help achieve public policy objectives, has been implemented vigorously for at least thirty years and is well established in the UK and Canada, and even more deeply rooted in the USA.

In more recent times rising government deficits and declining average real incomes have forced governments to assess critically the performance and resource claims of virtually all institutions associated with the welfare state. As a major public institution, the university has been asked to justify its public service performance, its demands for public resources, and the efficiency of its management of these resources. For most universities this was the first time they had been asked for a comprehensive accounting as public institutions. Most universities were unprepared to provide an effective response.

For the most part the university has attempted to justify itself in terms of the idealist notion of the university – academic freedom, the need for independence from external influences, the importance of developing new ideas through unconstrained curiosity-driven research, the value of a liberal education and related reasons – which in essence argue the university should not be held accountable by anyone other than itself. It has been defending the idea of the 'ideal' university from the past, or the small liberal arts college of the present, not the reality of the modern university as a major public institution of the late twentieth century. These arguments have been viewed by the providers of the massively expanded university funding (government and business) as self-serving, if not self-indulgent.

In addition, a significant amount of evidence has come to light documenting a fairly widespread poor performance of the university in managing the public resources at its disposal. Most universities simply gathered in resources from any and all sources without examining whether they compromised university independence or whether the university had the capability to perform at all, let alone efficiently and effectively. An increasing portion of those resources has been used to expand administrative overheads rather than teaching, research and other educational services. The university cultivation of students at both undergraduate and postgraduate levels, and the hiring of faculty, have reflected the resources that could be obtained at the moment, not long-term planning. This has tended to accentuate the business cycle in education and often to release maximum numbers of qualified graduates at the time of minimum demand for employment. Academic tenure has been used relatively little to preserve freedom from external interference on independent thinking, but far more to enforce internal regulation of thinking by the professions, to protect poor performance indefinitely and to insulate faculty positions from competition from the surplus postgraduates the universities faculties had produced.

In summary, for the most part the modern university has functioned primarily as an institution dependent on patrons and benefactors and has engaged only in short-term supply-side management. In contrast to the funding circumstances of small colleges, from which many universities have grown, the funding by university benefactors has been relatively short-term, not long-term. It has not been unconstrained funding to provide a liberal education, but rather based upon achieving public policy objectives. It has been subject to political influence and ultimately to an accounting for performance. What has developed during the generation in which the welfare state was constructed is the 'modern' university as a runaway bureaucracy. It had reached the limit of its expanding claim on public resources and, in the view of many people, was badly in need of reform.

## Reform of welfare state institutions

Most Western democracies are now in the throes of a reform of their welfare state institutions. The modern university, as a significant claimant on public resources, is part of it. These reforms are driven by different forces and objectives in different countries, but the overriding influence in all countries is that the state can no longer afford to pay the escalating claims, especially in light of the increasing internationalization of the economy. Some directions of change are clear: an increasing role for markets (privatization, deregulation, and so on), and a declining role for government; a scaling back of the social responsibilities government will assume, and the objectives and quality of its programmes; greater attention to applying cost–benefit analysis, establishing performance standards and exacting greater efficiency in the delivery of programmes; more detailed government monitoring, control and influence over the management of programmes. In essence, significant steps are being taken towards the corporatization of the university. In many cases this requires a corporate university administration with professionals from business, administration and fund-raising assuming positions formerly filled by academics. These are all steps towards what Innis described long ago as the 'mechanisation of knowledge' (Innis, 1951).

Despite the alarm from academics about the decline of the traditional idea of the university, the modern university has no real choice but to participate in this reform process. Now the university is firmly established as an institution whose primary mission is implementing public policies that bear on higher education. The reform of the university is all part of the decline and, in some areas, abandonment of the role of paternalistic government acting on behalf of the broader social and public interest needs of individual citizens (for instance, education and health) and society as a whole (environmental regulations, public broadcasting and anti-monopoly regulation).

In the liberalized economy, in many areas the role of government is shifting from provider of social and public services to independent arbiter of the claims advocated by different special interest groups. For example, in the UK, public utilities (electricity, water, telephone, gas) traditionally were supplied by public agencies under policies of universal service at reasonable and non-discriminatory prices. They were monopoly providers of essential public services. After privatization and liberalization these 'markets' are still highly monopolized. Following the US model, government regulatory agencies were established to oversee the industries. But the regulators are not advocates of social and public interest objectives. They tend to be arbiters of the special interests being advocated to them, primarily the utility and its large corporate consumers. Similarly, government departments (e.g. environment, food and drugs, and consumer protection), which used to undertake independent research to consider social and public policy implications, are being 'downsized' to the point where they must make decisions based primarily on assessments of research prepared to support advocacy positions being presented by different special interests. One of the responsibilities government is reducing significantly in the reform of the welfare state is independent applied research on the social and public interest implications of developments in many areas. Government is more and more the negotiating arena for special interests, and less and less the representative of the broader societal issues, those that are common to everyone but not the specific responsibility of anyone. In the reform of the welfare state, a question yet to be answered is, whither the public interest? Is a vacuum being created that the university can and should attempt to fill as part of a reconception of its role in the future, or might this simply aggravate the difficulties the university has run into already by allowing itself to become even more dependent on public policy-based funding (cf. Melody, 1990a)?

Its position must be to consider the nature of the future society in which the university will be functioning.

## The commodification of information

An ever more popular theme in the social sciences, as well as in the general literature over the past two decades, has been that technologically advanced economies are in the process of moving beyond industrial capitalism to information-based economies that will bring profound changes in the form and structure of economic, social, cultural and political systems. Rapid advances in computer and telecommunications technologies are making it possible to generate types of information that have been heretofore unattainable, transmit them instantaneously around the globe, and – in a rapidly growing number of instances – sell them in information markets. Some authors claim that the United States already devotes the majority of its economic resources to information related activities and will soon be an information society. The computer, telecommunications and information-content industries are among the most rapidly growing global industries, and are expected to remain so for the foreseeable future. The communications and information sector is a \$400 billion per annum global industry and represents nearly 20 per cent of world trade. Many national governments are counting on these industries to provide the primary stimulus to their future growth.

The state of information in the economy clearly has pervasive effects on the workings of the economy generally. It has intensified impacts on those sectors that provide information products or services, such as press, television, radio, film, mail, libraries, education, banks, credit bureaux, data banks and other 'information providers' as they are now called. And the establishment of information markets brings about changing conceptions of public and private information, as well as the property rights associated with marketable information in an information society.

In reality, of course, all societies have been information societies. The most significant change between technologically advanced society and the oral tradition of the Greek city-state – still practised by some cultures today – is not in the role of information in society, but in the way that information creation and exchange have shifted from oral discourse flowing outside the bounds of formal market arrangements to the establishment of institutions generating, storing and transmitting information, the commodification of information and its exchange through markets. Perhaps the most significant change is not the volume of information, but the structure, the distribution, the institutions and the dependence.

The stock of knowledge in society at any one time – the skills and education of the populace, the accumulated knowledge stored in universities, libraries and other institutions, the detailed factual information relating to such things as the workings of production processes, the interrelationships and interdependences of different sectors of the economy, and so on – collectively represent a primary resource of society. The value of this stock of knowledge to society depends on how pervasively it is spread throughout society, and upon the institutions for maintaining, replenishing and expanding the stock of knowledge – the education and training system, and research generating new knowledge.

Once information has been generated, the cost of replicating it is very much lower than the cost of generating it in the first instance. The consumption of information by one user does not destroy it, as occurs almost with all other resources and products. The information remains to be consumed by others, the only additional costs being those associated with bringing the same information and additional 'consumers' of it together under conditions where it can be 'consumed', or, more accurately, learned. And once a given level of penetration is achieved, a multiplier effect comes into play with many types of information, as the information is spread throughout society by informal communication processes outside the formal processes of learning and training. Hence, although the costs of adding to the stock of knowledge may be very great, there are generally significant economies in spreading that information throughout society, and so to other societies if the incentive exists to do so.

In the new age of information, much of the new information that is generated has its greatest economic value in scarcity rather than in widespread distribution. For example, information that has become important as a resource input to industrial, commercial and professional activities is specialized information often sought to provide 'inside' or superior knowledge. In essence, in imperfect economic markets, this inside information for private consumption strengthens the prestige, negotiation or market power position of the organizations or individuals that have access to it. Such information may or may not be costly to obtain, but its economic value clearly lies in its scarcity, that is, in the monopoly of information. Once such information becomes generally known to all interested parties, its economic value dissipates drastically.

Specialized information services for the private consumption of a restricted clientele are springing up daily. They range from the packaging and sale of government information and special research studies of the details of international markets for transnational corporations to confidential assessments of the negotiating strength of a specific customer, competitor, trade union or government. They include remote sensing satellite data identifying the detailed swimming patterns of schools of fish, pinpointing the location of mineral resources, as well as the progress of crop growth in distant countries. More and more funded research at universities carries restrictions on the ownership and use of the new knowledge generated. In the USA, researchers have been imprisoned for violating them.

Many governments have taken steps to attempt to restrict the march of information markets into the details of people's personal lives and to regulate the conditions of access to certain kinds of data banks – for example, credit, medical and tax files. The pursuit, sale and use of information in accordance with the incentives of the market-place clearly cannot be totally unrestricted. But the production characteristics of, first, the relatively high costs of establishing most data-base services, and second, the relatively low costs of extending the market for services already created, provide a powerful tendency towards centralization and monopoly on an international basis. Thus, competitive forces in many information markets are likely to be rather weak. This, in turn, can be expected to raise important issues of national and international government policy.

There is now a major task to which the education, public library and related institutions must attend. Historically, these institutions have assumed the major responsibility for expanding the information and knowledge accessible to the population at large. The continuing advance of information technologies and the spread of information services are facilitating a major restructuring of institutional relations in society. This will make it possible, and in some cases desirable, to bring certain kinds of information directly into the market-place. But in conjunction with these new information services, public information institutions must redefine their roles in meeting public information requirements in the evolving information society. This requires an assessment of what these needs are, as well as the best methods for delivering them so that access is as universal as possible. Given the very restricted budget conditions for public services in the foreseeable future, it will also require attention to the problem of cost recovery in a manner that will provide the minimal restrictions on public access.

Steps towards the increased commodification of information already have affected the university and the way it functions, including copying and the use of material, library and collection policies, access to libraries and electronic data bases, and intellectual property rights of faculty research, among others. Since 1994 commercial uses of the Internet have expanded greatly and it is now expected it will convert to commercial trading principles within the next few years. This will drive most unprofitable activities off the Internet and significantly restrict access by the imposition of prices where none exist now. International agreement on enforceable intellectual property rights is now a matter of top priority, as evidenced by the acrimonious US–Chinese trade negotiations on the subject over the last several years. The combination of (1) an order-of-magnitude increase in the mechanization of information and knowledge arising from applications of information technologies, (2) an exponential increase in the sheer volume of material produced, and (3) the application of economic market principles to monopolies of commodified information, will exert significant biases in shaping the knowledge environment – what is considered to be knowledge, and particularly valuable knowledge, and how it is disseminated.

These developments will play a major role in shaping the educational enterprise and the university of the future. Steps for major reforms through widespread automation (for example, computer-assisted learning, video lectures, electronic access to libraries and data bases) have already begun. The broadband information superhighway now under construction will provide the electronic communication capacity for an order-of-magnitude increase in the automation of the 'labour-intensive' educational services sector, including the university.

Clearly these changes strike at the foundations of the university – at the idea of the university, its roles and responsibilities, the conception and prioritization of types of knowledge, methods of research, training and the dissemination of knowledge. The objectives, direction, speed and priorities for transforming the education sector, and the role of the university in it, will be determined by public policies developed and implemented over the next decade. Should the university participate in the public policy debates on these issues? Should it adopt a comprehensive long-term research initiative to inform the policy debates and to ensure the broader public and societal implications are considered and the idea of an information 'commons' thoroughly examined? Should it attempt to arrive at a new conception of the appropriate role for the university in the information age? Should it advocate this role to public policy-makers as being in the best interests of society? To date the university has done none of these. It would seem to be in the university's self-interest and in the public interest that it does so.

## The university in an information economy

The university must be proactive in establishing a role for itself that stabilizes funding and preserves independent management, while providing positive contributions to implementing public policy in a manner consistent with university traditions. In the future the university will be operating in a very different economic and social environment. At least some of its major characteristics are evident. The extent of internationalization and globalization of activities will continue to grow. Competition among universities will increase on a world-wide basis. Education has been a major export in the UK for some time. Many universities in the UK, USA, Canada, Australia and a few other countries will become significantly more international, weakening their links with the education ministry, but strengthening them with the industry and trade ministries, as education is seen as a service with an almost boundless market to be tapped in 'newly developed' countries experiencing rapid economic growth and creating a middle class, especially in Asia.

Steps towards the commodification of information will be taken at a more rapid rate as intellectual property rights are standardized and extended to more countries, and new telecommunications networks (such as the Internet) are made more secure. Given the economic characteristics of information markets, which are supported by experience to date (for example, Chemical Abstracts, technical and legal data bases), there will be a strong tendency for information markets to become monopolies. The process of privatizing public information will be extended considerably.

The national and international economies will continue to become more interdependent, especially as the new telecommunication infrastructure – labelled by enthusiasts the information superhighway or the 'global information infrastructure' (GII) – is established and fully integrated into corporate trading relations. The market structure in most major industries already is gravitating towards 'tight oligopoly' (a few large international firms with enormous market power), a far cry from the invisible hand of competitive markets. This means markets will be extended only to consumers who will pay prices that provide a high level of profit. Many people will be excluded.

In this environment one can expect corporate entrepreneurs to 'prospect' for information and knowledge 'commodities' in the universities – libraries, laboratories, skills, professors, and so on – with a view to cherry-picking (asset-stripping in the trade) the potentially profitable activities. This will bring the university ever closer to integration with the rapidly developing information market-place, and reinforce the notion that the primary mission of the modern university is simply to do what its funders want it to do. It will be a unique institution because it has a core of special skills and services funded significantly by the state. University independence will tend to be eroded more and more. Its state funding base may become less secure. It will have no special mission or role that stamps it as making a unique contribution to society. In such an environment, can a university mission be fashioned that is consistent with the university public interest traditions?

Historically, certain industries have been recognized, both in custom and law, as 'business affected with a public interest'. These are businesses that supply services under conditions where the public is dependent upon reasonable and non-exploitable treatment by a business monopoly. They have included most public utilities, and the concept provides an indirect justification for regulating broadcasting. These industries are required by law to make their services universally available to the public, subject to reasonable and non-discriminatory prices and conditions. In the information society, access to certain kinds of information would appear to be the most essential public utility. Yet it would seem that the global information and communications industries may have outgrown the national institutional mechanisms for ensuring that the public interest is considered in their policies and practices.

The major deficiencies of public policy formulation today are an inadequacy of substantive research and analysis on the public interest implications of policy options, and an absence of effective advocacy of concrete policy actions that would reflect the public interest. The public interest perspective is that of society as a whole, focusing directly on the overall structure of benefits, costs and consequences for society. This perspective examines those consequences that lie outside the market calculations and the normal realm of special interest decision-makers, and includes an evaluation of economic externality, public good, as well as social and cultural consequences of policy options (cf. Anthony Smith, 1989; Melody, 1990b).

Perhaps more than any other policy area, information and communication policies require an overall systemic analysis of the long-term implications of the fundamental changes now in progress. They have enormous consequences for the development of an informed citizenry and the viability of political democracy, as well as economic and social relations of all kinds. The university is in a unique position to provide a substantial contribution to policy deliberations from a systemic perspective. The absence of a close connection with particular institutions that have a direct vested interest in the immediate results of policy considerations provides an essential detachment. This permits researchers to address the long-term economic and social implications of issues more thoroughly, independently and continuously than the policy-making agencies. In addition, by training and vocational practice, the perspective of independent researchers in the university should be more compatible with the long-run implications for society than that provided by any other institution. For many aspects of policy issues, the university can examine aspects of reality that elude special interest research and the normal analytical horizons of policy-makers.

But to be effective, the university will have to change its traditional role in three fundamental ways. First, it will have to extend the scope of its research and analysis to include the policy implications of its research findings. Unfortunately this is still a relatively rare practice. To do so, researchers will have to examine policy-making processes as an important component of their research. This should also impact teaching programmes providing an increased emphasis on public interest and societal theories, practices and implications.

Second, much greater attention will have to be paid to disseminating research results so they can be readily understood by the policy-making community. The objective would be to assess the significance of knowledge gained from research for policy development not only by government, industry and trade unions, but also by educational, social and other institutions.

Third, university researchers will have to become more involved in the policy development process, not only as first-hand observers, but also as periodic participants and advocates of the public interest implications of their research. Research has much more to contribute to policy issues than might at first appear. Across the social sciences in particular, there is a substantial amount of fragmented research on a variety of information and communication issues. An assessment of its significance for policy requires that it be pulled together, integrated and examined from a systemic perspective. The knowledge then needs to be interpreted in the light of major policy issues under debate. For the future, if the university can establish more effective research co-ordination, the knowledge gained can be more cumulative and less fragmentary. However, this will require that university researchers be as interested in convincing policy-makers as their peers.

If the role of the new university enterprise is extended to include societal implications of public policy issues, and if it is supported by strong programmes of dissemination, the benefits will begin to penetrate the social system more widely. Within the frame of this new model of the relation between the university and public policy, it should be possible to develop a much clearer understanding of the role of information in the information society and its implications for public policy, education (including the university), and economic and social development.

## Conclusion

In preparing itself for the decline of the welfare state and the transition to the information society of the future, the university must seriously reconsider its relation to, and participation in, public policy debate as part of a redefined educational mission. The reforms being applied to the university now are within the context of overall welfare state reform and involve more detailed control over funding and accountability for performance, as defined by state and business funders. This is resulting in a serious erosion of the independence of the university.

In the reform of the welfare state, government is significantly reducing its role in undertaking independent applied research on the social and public interest implications of developments in many areas. Government is becoming the negotiating arena for special interests rather than the representative of the broader societal issues that are common to everyone but not the specific responsibility of anyone. The university, as a societal, public interest institution, should consider the possibility of defining a role where it assumes responsibilities for a comprehensive examination of the societal and public interest implications of new and changing developments in society. Such a response can provide a positive response to the university's current dilemma and establish a role in the future information society that is consistent with its academic traditions.

## Notes

1. First presented as a paper, 'A Critical Review', to the Conference of Commonwealth Universities at Oxford, 23 July 1948.
2. In the decade after the Robbins Report, 1963–73, full-time university students in the UK almost doubled and full-time tenured faculty increased by more than 50 per cent (Dominelli and Hoogvelt, 1996, p. 72).

# 8

# Universities and Employers: Rhetoric and Reality

*Phillip Brown and Richard Scase*

## Changing careers

The relationship between higher education and employment in a post-industrial economy is undergoing fundamental change. In most advanced countries there has been a shift from an élite to a mass system of higher education. At the same time, both private and public sector organizations are being restructured in ways that challenge conventional assumptions about managerial and professional careers. Bureaucratic forms of organization which in the past offered careers through personal promotion and security of employment are being replaced by alternative organizational structures which are often described as *flexible, post-bureaucratic,* or *postmodern* (Brown and Scase, 1994). These changes in organizational structure challenge some of the fundamental assumptions that underwrite criteria of personal success in contemporary society.

The most significant change is to the idea of a 'career'. Wilensky suggests that, when viewed structurally, the 'career' can be defined as a succession of related jobs, arranged in a hierarchy of prestige, through which employees move in an ordered, predictable sequence. Corollaries are that the pattern of career progression is embedded and institutionalized in the structure of the organization and has some stability – the system is maintained over more than one generation of recruitment (Wilensky, 1960, p. 554). However, it is no longer possible for university graduates to plan their futures on a long-term basis. It is becoming increasingly difficult for them to assume that their work, and hence broader lifestyles, can be *anchored* within stable organizational structures of the kind that existed in the past. For virtually all employees the future consists of uncertainties and anxieties, and requires the ability to cope with the unpredictable nature of the world of work. Compared with earlier generations, today's university graduates are likely to experience periods of unemployment at various stages during their working lives. Forces of corporate restructuring are also likely to result in their moving more frequently between jobs within the same organization as well as making more frequent shifts between employers (Carnevale and Porro, 1994; Confederation of British Industry (CBI), 1994). Moreover, far more of today's graduates are likely to be found in self-employment, to be engaged in business start-up ventures and to be working in small businesses (Association of Graduate Recruiters, 1996).

Unlike the past, then, the occupational future of university graduates is characterized by both uncertainty and variety of work and employment experiences in what are becoming increasingly flexible and truncated careers. Hence graduates have to be more 'flexible' in their attitudes towards work and more 'adaptive' in their behaviour in the labour market. They require a broader portfolio of technical, social and personal skills than the more job-specific skills which were emphasized in the past. In earlier decades, graduates would leave universities to join employers who would train them to exercise specific organizational tasks on the basis of narrow technical expertise. The acquisition of technical expertise has not diminished, but organizations are now demanding that university graduates acquire such skills as part of a broader portfolio of personal competences.

This is not only a necessary requirement given the increasing emphasis on team and project approaches to work in innovative organizations, but also because the acquisition of generic skills is essential for graduate employees to maintain their *employability* in both the internal and external market for jobs. In place of bureaucratic careers, graduates are now required to have the necessary skills, experience and contacts to construct career portfolios, which will be inevitably contingent and unstable (Brown, 1995). Hence they need to be able to use their expert 'core' skills within a variety of work settings which, at various stages within their labour-market biographies, will incorporate working in both large and small businesses, and in companies that are constantly being rationalized and restructured because of global competition, technological innovation, corporate mergers and acquisition. At the same time, maintaining one's *employability* is also necessary to be able to trade as 'independent' and freelance consultants (Scase and Goffee, 1995).

## The decline of the bureaucratic career

The psychological and sociological consequences of these changes for university graduates are wide-reaching. In the past, notions of personal success and failure were closely based on age-related achievements (or not) in relation to such factors as organizational position, level of earnings and material standard of living. Hence evaluation of one's own personal performance – as well as that of others – could be based on a series of steps or stages which had to be achieved by certain ages in order to be regarded by oneself and by others as successful. Graduates could, therefore, 'benchmark' their achievements against others and also in relation to their own personal life plans (Mannheim, 1940).

Equally, from a sociological point of view, it was possible for graduates to 'plan' the nature of their personal relationships. Within a context of progression in a highly ordered future, they could plan various life-cycle patterns in terms of when to have children (and how many), whether or not to foster partner relationships, and how to plan projected (and reasonably predictable) earnings. In such a framework, graduates in relatively safe and clearly defined career jobs could make substantial financial commitments in terms of mortgages for house purchase and other long-term loans. The organizational career, therefore, was the pivotal axis around which middle-class lifestyles were structured (Whyte, 1965).

Indeed, it sustained the ideals of Western capitalism in nurturing the opportunity of social mobility for all, in which effort and talent would be rewarded both psychologically and materially. Accordingly, it legitimated wealth (achieved through personal career success) and poverty (for those who had failed in the meritocratic race). In the days of the cold war (1945–89), when Europe was divided between the countries of Western capitalism and Eastern European state socialism, the former was often portrayed as being morally superior because of its meritocratic, achievement-related rewards by comparison with the negotiation and sponsorship characteristic of state socialist regimes. Although these images owe more to rhetoric than to reality – as contrasting types of society – they were important as ideologies that sustained competing forms of social order for more than four decades. Moreover, meritocratic career progression within bureaucratic organizations played a key role in the social control of the middle classes: as Wilensky (1960, p. 555) has suggested, 'they give continuity to the personal experience of the most able and skilled segments of the population – men [*sic*] who otherwise would produce a level of rebellion or withdrawal which would threaten the maintenance of the system'.

However, such ideas of 'personal achievement' and 'career progression' have depended upon the bureaucratization of public and private sector organizations since the late nineteenth century (Gerth and Mills, 1958). It is this model of organizational efficiency which is presently breaking down, leading to a 'crisis' in the traditional assumptions, values and motivations of the middle class. Within the sociological literature most discussion of the nature of bureaucracy stems from the ideas of Max Weber. Weber argued that the growth of the modern organization was leading to the increasing bureaucratization of the world (Jacoby, 1973). By this he meant that large organizations were becoming increasingly structured according to a number of related principles. First, there is the clear delineation of work tasks so that all organizational participants know what is expected of them in terms of their duties and responsibilities. There are job descriptions, and people are expected to achieve their aims according to the procedures stipulated in these. Second, these jobs are hierarchically arranged so that organizational co-ordination is achieved through various reporting mechanisms leading to the delineation of roles of *superordination* and *subordination*. In other words, there are accountabilities whereby chains of command are organized in terms of control relationships. Third, the hierarchical structuring of specialized work tasks in bureaucratic organizations offers personal careers as part-and-parcel of the reward system. Appropriate performance is rewarded through promotion through the formally structured hierarchy. Equally, adequate performance requires personal commitment or loyalty, and this is obtained by offering organizational members relative security through (more or less) lifelong tenure (Merton, 1967). Further, the specialization of work tasks leads to skill enhancement such that both individual participants *and* the organization operate at an optimum level of efficiency. It was for this reason that Weber considered bureaucracies to be *rational* forms of organization compared with pre-industrial, traditional, forms of administration. But what happens when bureaucratic paradigms cease to be relevant for the structuring of organizations? What are the implications for the middle classes, and for university graduates in particular?

In bureaucracies, the overriding goal is to select those prepared to undertake tasks in a compliant, dutiful and reliable manner. Staff recruitment therefore focuses upon those who can demonstrate a willingness to play by the 'rules of the game', and who are able to co-operate with others in a functionally interdependent division of labour. They are not expected to be 'creative', 'entrepreneurial' or 'individualistic', since such behaviour undermines the essentially conformist cultures that bureaucracies require to be effective. Thus, there is an organizational requirement for mass recruits to lower-level positions where there is a demand for compliant employees in the *usual* bureaucratic manner. On the other hand, there is also a need for quite different sorts of person who have the potential to fill the top senior managerial positions. Such people do need to be creative and analytical in terms of their ability to formulate and implement organizational strategies. The result of this dual requirement is the emergence of a higher education system which, although structured on a unitary basis, is bifurcated in terms of this bureaucratic occupational order. What emerges in most advanced economies is an 'élite' group of institutions which provides the human resources for the senior organizational positions and a broader framework of institutions providing the training for those who will fill the great mass of technical, managerial and professional positions within bureaucratic structures. However, this neat fit between higher education and the occupational order becomes less relevant as organizations debureaucratize.

The shift to a 'flexible' paradigm of organization has been driven by a number of factors including a recognition that bureaucracy is inappropriate in an innovative environment; that 'downsizing' organizations could make substantial savings on labour costs, especially among the mass ranks of supervisors and middle managers; that job redesign and job enlargement not only made the organization more efficient but allowed greater potential for employers to exercise discretion, responsibility and creativity; that the widespread application of information technology allows organizational decision-making to be undertaken through non-human monitoring and communication processes. Hence the need for large numbers of compliant employees who undertake their tasks in a highly routinized and predictable manner is severely reduced. According to the flexible paradigm of organization efficiency, there is an increased need for those who are able to be creative within very ill-defined and ambiguous work settings. It is a form of organization that is decentralized on the basis of administrative units and operating processes. Each of these will be empowered to achieve its goals according to the most appropriate means. *Results* are monitored rather than *means*, and reward systems are structured accordingly. In the flexible organization there is a small core of key staff who may still be able to make a career within the organization, although this is likely to be truncated, involving horizontal as well as vertical mobility, given the absence of an extensive corporate hierarchy (Handy, 1989; Kanter, 1989). These core workers are supported by those on fixed or short-term contracts which offer little prospect of progression within the organization. Many of these workers are 'contracted in' when required and will include technicians and professional consultants. The flexible organization will also make extensive use of 'contracting out' to other companies which will undertake tasks previously provided in-house. Therefore, if the bureaucracy was characterized by stability and order, the flexible organization epitomizes constant change and uncertainty.

## From the 'bureacratic' to the 'charismatic' personality

As a result of these trends, employers state a preference for graduates who are able to cope with these new demands. They need employees with good interpersonal skills who are able to engage in 'rule-making' rather than 'rule-following' behaviour. What we are currently witnessing, therefore, is a significant change in the cultural capital required for entry into middle-class occupations (Bourdieu and Passeron, 1964). This change in cultural code can be summarized in terms of a shift from a 'bureaucratic' to a 'charismatic' personality (Brown and Scase, 1994; Brown, 1995). The idea of the charismatic personality is one which values those who seek to break the structures of routine actions and rule-following, to replace them with patterns of innovative and creative behaviour. 'The charismatic person is the creator of a new order as well as the breaker of routine order' (Shils, 1965).

The use of the term 'charisma' in this context differs from the idea of an élite of extraordinary people such as religious prophets, military heroes or political leaders. Our use of the term recognizes that the qualities of charisma are more attenuated and accessible to a much larger proportion of the population. In essence, the charismatic personality is the opposite to the bureaucratic in that it is primarily based on personal and interpersonal skills. The ability to get on with others and to identify with a strong corporate culture is paramount. Consequently, it is no longer enough to acquire the appropriate credentials and to show evidence of technical competence.

It is now the whole person who is on show and at stake in the market for managerial and professional work. It is the 'personality package' (Fromm, 1962), based on a combination of technical skills, qualifications and charismatic qualities, which must be sold.

This emphasis on the 'charismatic' personality package has come to assume increased prominence in the way employers recruit graduates in large and medium-sized organizations. In our interviews with 16 organizations – from retail banking, information technology, pharmaceuticals, leisure services, industrial manufacturing, accounting and local government – we found that employer recruitment criteria can be defined in terms of 'suitability', 'capability' and 'acceptability' (Brown and Scase, 1994).

## Suitability

The question of 'suitability' has traditionally been defined in technical terms, referring to the skills, knowledge and know-how necessary to 'get the job done' (Jenkins, 1985). However, given that the job to be done is likely to change radically and rapidly because of technological innovation, changes in product markets, and organizational restructuring and re-engineering, the criterion of suitability now incorporates communication, problem-solving and personal skills along with technical expertise. This is not to obscure the fact that the definition of 'suitability' will depend on the nature of the company in question and the specific job to be filled. For some occupations such as accountancy, marketing and personnel, the emphasis is almost exclusively on personal and transferable skills. In the scientific, engineering and research areas, although there is a greater emphasis on technical competence to do the job, there is no less a recognition that personal and social skills are a vital ingredient of performance, given an increased emphasis on teamwork, leadership and project management.

## Capability

Given that the organizations in which we conducted interviews were often keen to recruit graduates on to 'fast-track' training programmes, it is not surprising that they were also concerned about the 'capability' of candidates. This involved an assessment of 'raw talent', 'intellect' and 'quality of mind', which was primarily based on individuals' academic biographies at school, college and university. The need to recruit the 'best of the bunch' was motivated by a belief that it is the most intelligent people who are the most likely to deal successfully in an innovative setting because of their ability to see the bigger picture, and to subject problems to detailed analysis rather than having to rely on 'the way we've always done things'.

However, the criterion of capability is based not only on an assessment of the individual's innate intellectual ability, but also on whether he or she possesses that 'added something': the internal drive, energy, and ambition to 'make things happen', to be a 'shaper' rather than a 'follower'. Hence, there is a perceived need to recruit people who have determined their own fates in ways which are out of the ordinary, the assumption being that if they have shown evidence of those 'charismatic' qualities they will be more likely to be 'flexible', 'innovative' and 'enterprising'.

## Acceptability

Finally, the criterion of 'acceptability' concerns the degree of 'social fit' in terms of outlook, interests, connections, style, dress and speech, which provide the 'personal chemistry' required for a smooth transition into the organization's way of doing things. Acceptability, like suitability, has always been an important criterion of recruitment. However, in flexible organizations acceptability has assumed even greater significance for a number of related reasons. As social control within the organization comes to depend more on self-management (Rose, 1989) rather than on behavioural surveillance of the work process, the organization cannot function efficiently unless employees are willing to commit themselves to corporate goals (Peters and Waterman, 1982). Moreover, if work tasks are organized in teams, then it is essential that one recruits team-players. But being a team-player involves more than being willing to work with others; it also involves others being willing to work alongside the new recruit.

The criterion of acceptability also becomes more important in flexible organizations because the latter corrupt the integrity of the public and private as separate spheres of personal life (Merton, 1967). Employees are encouraged to view work as a way of life, rather than as a means of earning a living. Acceptability extends beyond an assessment of how the individual will perform 'from nine to five'. Whether the individual will fit into the social scene with colleagues after working hours becomes an important feature of acceptability in flexible organizations.

# Rhetoric and reality

If our description of the criteria of graduate recruitment is substantiated by further empirical investigation, it suggests that there is a contradiction between the rhetoric and reality of graduate recruitment. Although companies emphasize the need for people who are innovative, creative and self-motivated, there may in fact be less room for mavericks, loners, boffins or individualists, because of employer concerns about how 'personalities' fit into the changing interpersonal dynamics of the flexible organization. This suggests that although the shift to flexible forms of organization might be expected to lead to more 'pluralistic' approaches to corporate recruitment, in order to exploit the talents of graduates from different social, educational and ethnic backgrounds, as well as to the recruitment of a larger proportion of women, in reality the increasing importance attached to teamwork and project work becomes translated into the need for 'safe bets'; that is, people with the appropriate cultural capital (white, middle-class and frequently male).

Moreover, the more organizational efficiency is seen to depend on the interpersonal skills of communication, negotiation and teamwork, the more the bureaucratic legacy in schools, colleges and universities is seen by employers as a form of 'trained incapacity' (Merton, 1967, pp. 197–8). Academic qualifications tell employers less about what they need to know about potential recruits – their potential to work in teams or their social and personal skills – given that they convey information about their ability and motivation to jump through the appropriate examination hoops, to follow a course of prescribed study, and to regurgitate the key points under examination conditions, to recognize and defer to the authority of teachers and professors.

As a result there have been calls from employers to have a greater say in the affairs of the education system, in order to ensure that education provides enhanced business awareness, improved communication skills and self-management skills. The use of student 'profiling', for instance, which is intended to incorporate a broader range of student abilities, qualities and attainment than that typically assessed in academic examinations, is clearly an attempt to respond to employer rhetoric of personal and social skills. However, the use of student profiles has, as yet, had little impact on traditional patterns of 'bureaucratic' education (Brown and Lauder, 1992).

However, greater business involvement in education does not rule out the possibility of a growing contradiction between the classification and framing of knowledge, interaction and organizational practices operating in the educational system, and those found in employing organizations (Bernstein, 1975). Some of the reasons for this are not difficult to understand, and again they highlight contradictions, unintended consequences and 'forced' integration between education and the labour market rather than a structural 'correspondence' (Bowles and Gintis, 1976). Part of the problem is that group work has tended to be frowned upon because the democratization of educational opportunities has depended on the individuation of success and failure. Ability and performance, like the concept of meritocracy, is assumed to be judged on an individual basis. Group assessment, which could be introduced as a way of encouraging teamwork in a formal educational context, is also rejected given that it is difficult to evaluate when individual grades need to be assigned. Equally, a greater emphasis on the development of personal and social skills in education is also unlikely to gain widespread support, especially from the élite schools, colleges and universities. This is because the credibility attached to academic credentials remains based on the 'objective' assessment of 'knowledge' epitomized by the 'unseen' examination paper.

Therefore, as the market for graduate labour has become flooded through the rapid expansion of higher education, employers will increasingly target the élite 'old universities' on the grounds that they have the best intellectual talent, due to an assumption that because access is extremely competitive, only the best get in. Again, it should be noted that the extent to which employers will rely on the old universities will depend on the job in question. In jobs requiring specialized vocational training, the new 'mass' institutions of higher education are able to compete with the élite institutions by tailoring the curriculum to meet the technical needs of large companies. Nevertheless, the proliferation of initiatives, especially in the 'new' universities, which aim to furnish students with the personal and social competences required by flexible organizations may do little to enhance the job chances of their students. Undergraduates, in the 'new' universities, are encouraged to develop their 'leadership' and 'teamwork' potential, while at the same time being more 'creative' and 'entrepreneurial' in their approach to studies. Courses have become more project-focused, requiring students to exercise their ability to work both independently and in co-operation with others. However, despite these attempts by the institutions of 'mass' higher education to nurture such skills, these graduates continue to be perceived by employers as lacking the necessary cultural capital (Brown and Scase, 1994). Indeed, such initiatives are viewed by employers as the latest version of 'compensatory' education for disadvantaged students evident in the 1960s and 1970s. Hence, instead of opening up opportunities to traditionally disadvantaged youth, the expansion of higher education has involved an assessment by employers that 'more means different' (Ball, 1990), exaggerating the existing hierarchy of academic worth which favours the élite universities.

This is not to argue that university education is worthless and that those from less privileged backgrounds do not benefit or enhance their market value by studying for degrees. Clearly, the greater majority do, if only because it provides routes into the labour market whereby employment in low-paid, unskilled jobs can be avoided, albeit often after their studies are complete, given problems associated with financing tertiary education. But it does mean a degree is no longer the key which will open doors into well-paid, senior organizational positions. These remain 'earmarked' for those with the cultural capital that is difficult to acquire without attending élite institutions of higher education. Hence the often stated claim by employers that, while they would like to select graduates from a broad university base, their experience confirms that it is only in the élite universities that they are able to find the type of person that suits their corporate needs (Brown and Scase, 1994).

# A portfolio of jobs

There is a further issue which needs to be elaborated in light of corporate restructuring and demise of graduate careers, given that the changes we are describing have wider implications than initial occupational recruitment. This is because the implicit contract of job security for loyalty between white-collar workers and employers has been broken. The CBI (Confederation of British Industry) report on graduates for twenty-first-century employment, for instance, noted that the 'traditional template of the "graduate job" is disappearing. Its replacement is characterised by uncertainty, permanent change and absence of hierarchy. A graduate career is now a portfolio of jobs – and skills – rather than a job for life.' (CBI, 1994, p. 13; Watts, 1996). This change in the nature of middle-class careers is invariably defined as a technical problem of how to teach workers to be flexible, adaptable and self-reliant.

Our study of graduate orientations to the labour market in the early 1990s adds weight to the argument that the vast majority of students are ill prepared for the corporate realities of the 1990s. The dominant orientation shared by these students was what we described as 'traditional bureaucratic'. This orientation was based on making a long-term commitment to the organization, which in turn would provide incremental career progression. The tradition bureaucratic career is premised on a regular and predictable climb in the organizational hierarchy, bringing with it increases in salary, status and responsibility, rather than the development of a labour-market portfolio involving regular job changing or self-employment.

A much smaller proportion of students held 'flexible' orientations to future employment. Here occupational careers were perceived in terms of frequent job changes in the development of career portfolios and a 'value-added' curriculum vitae rather than through progression within bureaucratic hierarchies. Pertinent to this discussion was the fact that the vast majority of those with 'flexible' orientations were from the élite of the three universities included in this study and most were men. Therefore, rather than the development of career 'self-reliance' (Waterman *et al.*, 1994) being a technical issue concerning the reform of education, or a matter of developing the 'right' personal psychology, the development of traditional bureaucratic rather than flexible orientations to the labour market in the 1990s may more accurately reflect perceived differences in labour-market power.

Hence, rather than viewing the vast majority of students as having an inadequate understanding of the labour market in the 1990s, the opposite may prove to be a more accurate interpretation. The reason why most students in this study, who did not attend Oxbridge, maintained a 'traditional bureaucratic' rather than a 'flexible' orientation was that they had a realistic understanding of their relative labour-market power. Many of these students knew that it was going to be very difficult to get on to a fast-track training scheme with a reputable organization. This led them to define their main task as gaining entry to such an organization which would then offer them a labour-market shelter (Ashton, 1986) from what was increasingly seen to be a cut-throat competition within which they lacked a competitive advantage. This was particularly evident among students from working-class backgrounds, ethnic minorities and a large proportion of women. Two of the Asian and Afro-Caribbean students interviewed believed, for instance, that traditional bureaucratic careers provided shelters from discrimination in the competition for jobs. Some of the female students also viewed traditional bureaucratic routes as a possible solution to the impending conflict between 'career' and 'family'. Whereas it was recognized that starting a family and pursuing a career would be very difficult to manage if career progression was based on moving from job to job, it was assumed that the interruption which child rearing inevitably entailed would be less damaging in terms of a career in traditional bureaucratic organizations. This was especially when they saw themselves as being able to depart from employment for future child rearing, and then to return, in some cases only part-time, in the classic female pattern (Crompton and Sanderson, 1990).

Indeed, in bureaucratic forms of organization, it is possible for those who are not on the 'fast track' to senior management positions to protect themselves from potential sources of *organizational insecurity*, certainly by comparison with their counterparts employed in organizations we have described as 'flexible' or post-bureaucratic. By definition, bureaucratic organizations have clearly defined rules and procedures stipulating hiring and firing, promotion procedures and staff appraisal. Often, these are associated with the establishment of committees that are bestowed with the authority to implement procedures in accordance with the prescribed rules. Further, such committees often incorporate representatives of employees, particularly within public sector organizations, or the procedures are implemented according to what are perceived to be legitimate and fair practices. As a result, 'arbitrary' management decision making is reduced as is the capacity for managers to exercise personal discretion and judgement in relation to human resource policies. Indeed, a key driver of debureaucratization has been the attempt by management groups to break down restrictive and cumbersome working and procedural practices associated with employee relations and human resource management.

However, within flexible organizations, the abolition of such rules increases the vulnerability of employees. They have less capacity to appeal to formally prescribed rules and procedures and they are more prone to the arbitrary and discretionary judgement of their managers. The direction of organizational change is reinforcing this; companies are not only debureaucratising but also 'decentralizing' and breaking up their reporting structures. Consequently, many organizations are adopting 'federate' structures which incorporate a number of relatively autonomous business units. Sometimes these may be constituted as subsidiary companies or, alternatively, as profit-and-loss or budget centres. But whatever form they take, there is a transformation in management practice from bureaucratic to flexible which, by definition, entails the abandonment of rule-bound behaviour and reinforced emphasis upon personal discretionary decision making. In other words, the organization becomes a federation with each cost-centre leader competing for corporate resources in order to develop or protect his or her own particular segment of the overall business.

In such circumstances, those responsible for these operating units are extended organizational autonomy such that they are able to introduce their own human resource strategies in relation to selection, promotion and the allocation of rewards. They are able to develop their own organizational 'cultures' according to which appropriate and inappropriate behaviour can be nurtured and sanctioned. Thus they are able to introduce their own criteria of 'leadership potential', personal effectiveness and 'interpersonal skills'. A possible outcome is the fostering of cultures that encourage compliant and conformist behaviour – according to the dictates and stipulations of the senior managers of these business units – despite the cultivation of *rhetoric* that emphasizes personal creativity, empowerment and personal growth. In other words, the post-bureaucratic, decentralized form of organization becomes characterized by 'personal patronage' and 'personal sponsorship' of the sort associated with the patron–client relations of the Mafia.

It is, then, hardly surprising that those lacking in cultural capital can find themselves disadvantaged in such flexible forms of organization. On the other hand, those who have attended 'élite' institutions of higher education, with their greater understanding of the subtleties of interpersonal relations, are potentially better equipped to manipulate these for their own personal ends. Hence, the emergence of the flexible organisation can lead to employee feelings of inequity and unfairness (V. Smith, 1989) and to the reproduction of class-related privileges and disadvantages within the organization (Scase, 1992). It is little wonder, then, that women and other historically deprived groups express an explicit preference for working within bureaucratic forms of organization (Goffee and Scase, 1989).

## Reputational capital

Of course, all this presupposes that the role of the university system *is* to prepare people for employment, whether they be school leavers or, increasingly in a postindustrial society, those who are already in the labour market. Indeed, this is a questionable assumption despite attempts by governments to introduce policies to make university education more relevant to the needs of industry. Certainly, the role of higher education is becoming increasingly ambiguous as a result of broader societal transformations. Compared with only a couple of decades ago, universities have lost their position as monopoly providers of knowledge in a number of areas, particularly within the humanities and the social sciences. It is no longer necessary to leave home, to rent uncomfortable accommodation and get a low-paid, part-time job while attending university to understand, for example, issues of social and economic inequality. The traditional mode of delivery of such information via the 50-minute lecture is now challenged by information technologies which are able to offer various forms of distance learning through the use of multimedia computers, teleconferencing and the Internet.

Moreover, in the mid-1970s there were few social scientists working in the media. Today, most newspaper, magazine, television and radio journalists, editors and producers will have studied at least some of the social sciences while at university. With the use of media technology, they have been able to build on their own knowledge and 'beat the universities at their own game'. Those interested in poverty and inequality, for example, can often obtain more up-to-date information and analysis through newspapers, magazines and computer databases than from academic books and journals. Even in the natural sciences, developments in information technology are destroying the need to attend university. The growing use of such innovations as the Internet could enable students to construct a broad portfolio of courses selected from those offered by eminent professors on a worldwide basis. The learning process can be undertaken on an interactive basis *without* the need for face-to-face relations in a specific geographical location. Hence, the seminar room, the lecture theatre and the university campus are no longer a necessary condition for in-depth academic study.

So why have universities expanded precisely at the time when the monopoly of academic knowledge is most under threat? The reason is simply that the transmission of knowledge is only a part of the university's role in society. Perhaps of equal importance is the fact that universities have largely maintained a monopoly over the award of high-status credentials. Indeed, so long as universities can maintain a monopoly over the examination process, where and how students learn is of diminishing importance. Universities have become key players in the provision of distance learning and the franchising of course materials, if not the university's imprimatur, to institutions around the world. What is crucial to universities is that they maintain or seek to enhance their 'reputational' capital in order to maximize the market value of their products (diplomas, BAs, MScs, PhDs) relative to the 'branded' certificates of other higher education institutions. After all, what is important to students in the competition for jobs is how an individual is judged relative to others. If only 5 per cent of the population have a university degree, it matters far less what reputational capital is attached to the qualification than in a situation where 30 per cent of labour-market entrants have an equivalent qualification.

Hence, although a university education can offer the prospect of a middle-class 'career' to a reduced proportion of students in higher education, there is little to suggest that the demand for higher education will decline in the coming decades. The decline of bureaucratic careers and the absence of employment security mean that a university education offers the opportunity to avoid long-term unemployment or a life in low-waged, low-skilled work. To express this more formally, investment in tertiary education has become a form of 'defensive' expenditure, especially for those who have not gained access to élite colleges and universities. Thurow and Lucas suggested that 'education becomes a good investment, not because it would raise an individual's income but because it raises their income above what it will be if others acquire an education and they do not' (cited in Hirsch, 1977, p. 51).

A further expansion of higher education can also be anticipated because it offers governments in postindustrial societies a partial solution to youth unemployment. With the increasing application of information technology modern societies require less in the form of human labour. Accordingly, not only are rates of unemployment likely to continue to be high beyond the year 2000, but also there is less need for individuals' working years to be as extensive as they were in the past. In order to reduce the demand for labour-force participation, therefore, university participation delays entry into the labour market just as early retirement fulfils a similar function for older age groups. Indeed, access to higher education for young people keeps alive the meritocratic ideal of a middle-class career.

For older or more mature students, universities offer opportunities for retraining and career change. But equally as important is their role for the purposes of *identity reconstruction*. They offer a context within which mature students are able to 'step out' of their everyday taken-for-granted identities and review their life experiences. It is not surprising, therefore, that for some of these students attending university is associated with the break-up of partner relationships and the reconstitution of personal networks, cultural interests and socio-political activities. Hence, although access to higher education can have significant benefits associated with individual self-development, the nurturing of middle-class occupational aspirations at a time when these are likely to remain extensively unfulfilled suggests that in the next decade the problem of 'over-education' will become a major political issue.

That we remain some way from a 'virtual' university system is also explained by the fact that the mode of transmission and the social context in which it takes place are often as important as curriculum content. As employers in flexible organizations emphasize personal and social skills, the university as a 'finishing school', nurturing the appropriate forms of cultural capital, has become even more important to students aspiring to enter professional and managerial 'careers'. The importance of the university as a source of social education was clearly recognized by mature students in the study of higher education and corporate restructuring cited above (Brown and Scase, 1994). They realized that having to leave the campus after lectures in order to fulfil work and family obligations deprived them of the opportunity to socialize with other students and develop contacts which could prove to be extremely useful once they enter the labour market. Hence, a key role of campus universities is to manufacture personal and social identities which modern learning technologies cannot supersede.

In conclusion, it can be suggested that the relationship between systems of higher education and the occupational orders of advanced economies are increasingly ambiguous, despite attempts to make the former more vocationally relevant. The growth of flexible organizations has reinforced the divide between 'élite' and 'mass' forms of higher education. Notwithstanding this, they have fulfilled other sociological as well as psychological functions which have emerged as modern society has evolved from the stage of industrialism to the age of information. But, with the exception of the most prestigious institutions, they may no longer be the gateway to social mobility that they were in the past!

# 9

# Conclusion:
# An Affirming Flame

*Anthony Smith and Frank Webster*

## Image versus reality

In the UK the word 'university' readily evokes an image of changeless tradition: ancient buildings and unworldly intellectuals surrounded by students whose chief interests are dining clubs, sports, and old school ties. Consider, for example, the television serializations of Evelyn Waugh's *Brideshead Revisited*, Fredrick Raphael's *Glittering Prizes*, and Tom Sharpe's *Porterhouse Blue*, or the films *Shadowlands*, *Chariots of Fire* and *True Blue*, and you will get the picture. An entire raft of novels, whether celebratory or detracting, supports this vision (Carter, 1990).

In fact, however, most British universities are less than 30 years of age (Scott, 1995), very few indeed existed a century ago, all have long-term and close relationships with the wider society (cf. Sanderson, 1972), and students are quite different from their media stereotypes. Today it is much more usual for the student to be enrolled at an institution situated in a large metropolitan city and taking business studies than at a collegiate or campus university and reading philosophy. This contrast between image and reality also alerts us to another important feature of universities – they have never been a fixed entity, frozen in form. Quite the contrary: universities have been ever changing, always adapting to new circumstances, whether it be introducing new curricula in English literature and the natural sciences in the nineteenth century or endorsing a principle of meritocracy shortly after the Second World War when a decisive move was made towards admitting students on the basis of achievement in examinations (Carswell, 1985).

Moreover, there never was a uniform type of university institution, whatever the popular image might conjure. Thus Oxbridge coexisted with redbrick universities such as Leeds and Leicester, with their own habits and procedures. Later these were joined by the new out-of-town campus universities of the 1960s such as Sussex and Kent, along with the former colleges of advanced technology such as Brunel and Surrey, each bringing distinctive orientations. Later still these were joined by the former polytechnics, which in 1992 were retitled universities and started to shift their emphases, though they brought along particular concerns such as with access and especially close relations with the world of work. Perhaps there was a brief period, between the Robbins Report and the end of the 1970s, when a particular idea of the university was hegemonic (that is, ideologically endorsed and aspired towards) which emphasized the ideals of a residential academic community and intimacy between students and academic staff, but, looking back, we may appreciate that this was an interregnum in a long history of change, adaptability and difference within the university sector.

Lately it may be especially important to be reminded of this since the cascade of changes enveloping higher education can be regarded all too readily as an overturning of all that has gone before. We do not want to underestimate what the shift from élite to mass higher education portends, but if we bear in mind that continuous development and adaptation are implicit in a differentiated university system, then we are likely to be sceptical of the more extravagant interpretations of today's changes.

No one reading this book will be unaware of the range and diversity of recent trends in higher education: a huge leap in student numbers coinciding with unceasing reductions in funding; a visibly declining university infrastructure which is in urgent need of renovation and which is, in many cases, architecturally inappropriate for handling the large numbers of students that today are routine; a significant diminution of the standing and status of academics; an emphasis on the vocational dimensions of university education; a culture of audit and assessment, all in the name of greater accountability to the public paymaster; a decisive shift away from collegial forms of governance towards distinctively managerial methods; a bewildering number of new arrangements introduced to facilitate and encourage working with outside agencies; an astonishing growth of new subject areas and associated knowledges; an almost universal conversion to modularization of undergraduate programmes . . .

These and other changes have placed enormous pressures on the university system. They have certainly resulted in a noticeable shift in the 'feel' of university life. For many academics this has been experienced as an appreciable loss of control over what they do, initiatives coming from the central management teams that drive the organization and from politicians from without the university. A result is that institutions are experienced more as places of 'work' than the community of scholars which motivated many academics to choose their vocation.

Students, too, are significantly different from those of a generation ago. Expanding numbers so rapidly while simultaneously cheapening the unit of resource has not only crowded campuses with new constituencies, but also reduced the individual attention given to those students, making learning more anonymous and self-determined. With this goes a decline in the intimacy between students and their teachers which has been for many a defining feature of higher education in the past. And with the loss of intimacy goes a decline in satisfaction and purpose.

Moreover, there is evidence that many students, if nominally full-time, are in effect part-time students, since they feel compelled to work (in bars, restaurants, offices, etc.) to supplement an increasingly inadequate grant. Recent research from the Policy Studies Institute, for example, suggests that fully one-third of all students work continuously (and most intermittently) during their undergraduate years (Callender and Kempson, 1996). It seems logical to many observers that educational standards must be declining in the face of this, though degree results appear to proclaim the contrary. Nowadays more students than ever – indeed about half of all candidates – graduate with an upper second or a first class honours degree, though it was less than one in three 20 years ago. But there are many who doubt the raw statistics of degree classifications. They contrast the modest entry qualifications of many students with their achievement in final assessments, are sceptical of claims of massive 'added value' injected by universities, and explain the formal maintenance of standards – in the face of curtailment of opportunities to study, poorer facilities for learning, and less contact with teachers – with reference to a general easing of assessment, a massive tilt away from unseen examinations towards course work, and evidence of variable standards between universities (cf. Higher Education Quality Council, (HEQC), 1996a; 1996b; Gibbs *et al.*, forthcoming).

It is tempting, confronting this transformation from élite to mass higher education and all the attendant pressures of squeezed resources and greater external direction, to give up on it all. As solace, the appeal of a Golden Age, one of small classes, high standards, well-prepared students, and generously funded and autonomous institutions, is compelling.

# Achievements

## Access

Whatever its appeal, nostalgia must be tempered with a full appreciation of at least two major achievements of the move to mass higher education. Above all, there is much to applaud in the opening up of opportunities for participation that expansion has allowed. To be sure, a participation rate of even one in three of the age group still leaves room for improvement, but compared with even the recent past it is to be applauded that doors have been thrown open for so many who would formerly have been excluded from academe. Moreover, the easing of entry barriers, enabling many mature students to attempt higher education, while it has placed some additional strains on the university, has undoubtedly been an advance, introducing into the university a sizeable proportion of people whose experiences and orientations can deepen the education of the rest while at the same time giving those who as school leavers missed out on university a chance to achieve at degree level.

When we celebrate this extension of opportunity we are not unmindful of the down side, to which Phil Brown and Dick Scase refer in the previous chapter, of a reduction in what a degree qualification now commands by way of employment. It is clearly the case that, there being now many more candidates who possess university degrees competing for job vacancies, these qualifications do not guarantee – as once they did – a middle-class occupation. In addition, there is the reality that job patterns are more and more insecure and changeable (in the current jargon, 'flexible'). Obviously there is a problem in the match between student expectations and the sorts of career that will be open to them. Many graduates of today's universities are on course to meet with disappointment, sooner rather than later, in their working lives.

Our reason for celebration thus does not lie in the inflation of credentials that mass higher education has induced. It is found much more in the intrinsic elements that come from the opening of university doors, in the personally transformative dimensions of immersion in higher education, in the intricate processes of identity formation and reconstruction, to which all who work in, and all who have been through, the university may testify (cf. Boyer, 1987). Such qualities are not readily measured in the performance indicators which bedevil higher education today. And this is not because questions such as 'what is your graduate employment rate six months after finals?' ought not to be put. It is rather that they so narrow what university life is about – to all involved – that we may too readily fail to appreciate fully these major benefits, manifest but extraordinarily hard to quantify, of university expansion.

Certainly the increased access that has come about does not mean that today's students experience the same education as their forebears of a generation ago. Classes now are too big for individual consideration, tutors too hard pressed to give sufficient personal attention, research pressures too acute to allow teaching the priority it merits, and libraries too over-stretched to provide the resources once available, to replicate what used to be offered. Nevertheless, opportunities to experience the higher learning have been massively expanded against the odds in recent years, and this has undeniably been a force for good, as systematic research demonstrates (cf. Pascarella and Terenzini, 1991) and as conversation with groups of what are euphemistically called 'non-traditional' students will show (cf. Caul, 1993).

## Pedagogy

A second gain that ought to be noticed lies in pedagogy. There has always been some inspired teaching at university level, but it has not been a requirement that university academics demonstrate capability to teach as well as to conduct research. Even now it is relatively rare for appointment panels to ask for certification of teaching ability from candidates, but it is at least common to consider a capacity to teach as a requirement of a job offer (cf. Astin, 1993).

The past couple of decades have marked real advances in the knowledge and practice of teaching and learning. The novice university teacher no longer need be left to take his or her first class unaided, advised – if given any advice – to rely on a combination of enthusiasm, knowledge and force of character. There are now available authoritative guides on how to teach effectively, how best to improve learning, on how students should organize and orient towards their studies (Gibbs, 1996). Partly, no doubt, this has been of necessity in response to the entry of new types and numbers of university students and the resultant pressures to cope. Partly also it reflects the fact that so very little university research time has been given over to researching higher education teaching in the UK. It has been pioneered especially by the former polytechnics, which from the outset had a brief to concern themselves more with teaching than with research. Whatever the causes, this prioritization has had widespread and noticeable effects – for instance, in a shift away from reliance on 'lecture and reading list' forms of teaching; in changed forms of assessment that are more appropriate techniques of evaluation than ten or so unseen three-hour examination papers in year three; in a plurality of teaching strategies; and, more generally, in much more thoughtfully produced and student-centred course materials.

These sorts of development have come about, on the whole, by a mix of informal as well as more institutionalized mechanisms such as the the spread of 'good practice' among colleagues through personal networks, external examiner links, professional bodies, and validation panels. The recent introduction of Teaching Quality Exercises may have been flawed, and they certainly seem to have been regarded as an imposition by many departments, but the reliance on a large pool of peers as assessors – who will take back to their own, and around to other universities, knowledge of strengths and weaknesses in teaching and learning – of their colleagues' work will surely encourage improvement in these areas.

Though there remains a great deal still to be done, improvements in pedagogy are palpable in universities today. At the least now students will be provided with clear course aims and objectives of their degree programmes when, and even before, they arrive at the university; learning outcomes will be articulated at the outset of a course and its assessment explicit linked to what students are expected to learn; course guides are now a great deal more than undifferentiated lists of book and journal titles; well-prepared class handouts are routine; students' induction into information resources and study habits at university level is carefully considered and frequently built into the formal curriculum; and assessment tasks evidence serious thought having been given to students' learning. Such improvements in teaching and learning are at least one reason why standards of achievement among students have been maintained, and even improved, despite massive increases in participation rates without additional resource provision (cf. Lucas and Webster, 1997).

# The postmodern university?

To identify positive consequences of the development of mass higher education is antipathetic to some since they see little but a grand decline (cf. Bloom, 1987; Hirsch, 1987). We shall return to these objections below, but for now will spend some time considering the most radical interpretation of what is taking place. A diverse group of thinkers, represented here in the contributions of Zygmunt Bauman and Peter Scott, suggest that higher education is not simply adapting, but is rather transmuting, into a radically new phenomenon, the postmodern university. In this scenario it is not just a matter of teaching more students on fewer resources, or of paying more attention to alternative sources of university income, or vainly trying to maintain standards in a tumultuous time. The changes are altogether more fundamental, such that the postmodern university bears little resemblance to what went before. This new university is decidedly heterogeneous, so much so that the title 'university' indicates little if anything by way of common institutional features. Consonant with this, within any university heterogeneity predominates, such that between departments, and even within them, colleagues can scarcely make sense of one another, so radically separate are their specialisms and the discourses that each has constructed.

Such thinkers have conceived this as a transformation of knowledge, a move away from what may be termed Mode 1 knowledge which is homogeneous, rooted in strong disciplines which are hierarchical, and transmitted to novitiates in an apprentice–master relationship, to Mode 2 knowledges which are non-hierarchical, pluralistic, transdisciplinary, fast changing, and socially responsive to a diversity of needs such as students' dispositions and industrial priorities (Gibbons *et al.*, 1994; cf. Lyotard, 1993). This plurality of knowledges announces an end to established and common purposes of the university, there being no identifiable unity and no possibility of agreement on goals or even methods of work.[1]

Instead there is a multiplicity of *differences*: different academics pursuing different knowledges, different teams of researchers combining and recombining to investigate shifting topics, different sorts of students following different courses, with different modes of study and different concerns among themselves, different employment arrangements for different types of staff – difference everywhere in this the postmodern, flexible, accommodating university.

As a description of what is happening in the university a good deal of this rings true. Significantly, some observers who may not altogether share the positive vision of Professors Bauman and Scott still agree on much of the empirical description. The late Bill Readings (1996), for instance, regarded the widespread proclamations of university leaders that they achieve 'excellence' in a bewildering range of different areas – in student union facilities, in academic research, in associations of former students, in sports halls, in car parks, in teaching, in committee structures, in equal opportunities – as a signal that the search for, still less agreement on, unifying purposes of higher education has been abandoned in favour of an out-and-out relativism wherein anything and everything can be equally 'excellent'.

The enthusiasm for 'multi-vocalism' and our 'good fortune' to find it in the university today was not shared by most of those participating in the Fulbright colloquium from which this book comes. On the one hand, there remained a deep commitment to recognizably Enlightenment ideals from many of those present – more Mode1 knowledge than Mode 2. Thus Michael Ignatieff spoke of the endeavour to develop 'humane scepticism' in students, something that has foundations in tools of analysis and knowledges heavily dependent on disciplinary traditions. It is a theme returned to in Paul Filmer's (Chapter 5) advocacy of the principle of disinterestedness where this is developed as a foundational principle of every university. Such arguments, which are essentially modernist, have their roots in Ruskin, Arnold and Newman.

On the other hand, the heterogeneous university is to be resisted on grounds that it underestimates – and this ironically – the realities of the *hierarchies of difference* within and between universities. It is all very well to claim the common title 'university' for in excess of 100 institutions in Britain today, and it is superficially appealing to contend that each is distinguished from all others (as well as being internally fractured). But while this highlights the complexities of locating universities on matrices of difference, it is an absurdity – and one that is ultimately injurious, especially to students – to suggest that differences are such as to subvert hierarchy. Postmodernists may resist judgement, but employers, students, academics, and indeed the public as a whole, do not (Brown and Scase, 1994). The upshot is that, while judgement has its gradations and grey areas, universities as a whole, and in turn departments and subject areas, are accorded a place. Here there is little doubt about the location of institutions such as Oxford, Cambridge and Imperial College, more hesitancy when it comes to Liverpool and Newcastle, but a return in confidence of judgement as regards the likes of Bolton and Derby. Of course, such judgements are more nuanced when it comes down to particular disciplinary areas or to specific needs of certain students, but acknowledgement of the difficulties of judging differences does not negate the fact of their hierarchical nature. As Alan Ryan (1996) bluntly puts it, 'everyone knows it, but it is felt indecent to say so'.

It is not some sort of blind snobbery to recognize such hierarchies, just as it is not the prejudice of subject panels which assess research outputs and teaching provisions at periodic intervals. It is, as Brown and Scase forcefully argue (Chapter 8), a realist position which it is essential to endorse if the issue of *social justice* is to be addressed. In the world of employment a degree from Cambridge carries more weight than one from pretty well anywhere else in Britain (cf. Purcell and Pitcher, 1996). Research activities undeniably are maintained at a higher level in some institutions than in others. Arguably too assessment standards are less rigorous in some institutions than in others (HEQC, 1996b). It is right that one qualifies judgements when it comes to particular people in particular circumstances, but to ignore such differences is to turn a blind eye especially to the social inequalities that are inherent in higher education. If these are to be tackled, then what must be achieved is at once a refusal of the rampant relativism (and phony egalitarianism that often goes with this) of postmodernism which announces difference as an excuse to avoid judgement, and a simultaneous rejection of a knee-jerk 'more means worse' mentality which refuses to discern nuance and change within the education system.

## The death of the university?

There has been a good deal of comment recently speculating on the decline, even the death, of the university as an institution. As a rule three arguments are adduced in support of this claim. First, there is the emergence of alternative sources of knowledge which undermine the university's monopolistic position. The development of the Internet in particular, but also the spread of multimedia technologies and even cable television, are frequently highlighted in this regard. Beyond the walls of established higher education institutions, floating in cyberspace, one may find discussion groups, research networks, bulletin boards, and associated forms of the emergent 'virtual university'.

Second is the related matter of changing ways of teaching and learning. Why, it is asked, visit the university to learn when one may connect, at one's own convenience, to on-line data bases from office or home for at least as rich, and arguably richer, sources of instruction? In turn this raises the wider issue of the spread of distance learning, a movement which overcomes the limits of space imposed on gaining a traditional university education, while also allowing – at least potentially – any student to get on-line access to the leading figures in any given field. If MIT or Imperial College engineering courses can be packaged and made available via information and communications technologies then, arguably, many other established university departments of engineering can be dispensed with, or at the least drastically reduced, and replaced with a superior study programme from a more prestigious institution. The rapid spread of franchising is an indication of just this trend, albeit at a more modest level. Thus, increasingly, one can study for a degree many miles away from the awarding body, or one might have the first year delivered by teachers in a local further education college far away from the host university.

Third, the university's location as the privileged source of research provision is being weakened by the emergence and success of alternative sites such as think-tanks, corporate research and development laboratories, research institutes and government agencies. Some of these have been around for years, but in recent decades they have grown in strength and have had a marked effect. The likes of Demos, the Institute of Economic Affairs, and the Adam Smith Institute in Britain (and there are many more similar organizations in North America) are indicative of this trend which breaks down the previously privileged doors of the university (Cockett, 1994). Most striking of all are the research arms of corporations such as British Telecom, ICI and AT&T, where multi-billion-dollar budgets are committed annually for the employment of literally thousands of post-doctoral candidates (and several Nobel prize winners), whose working conditions seem much the same as those found inside universities (apart from higher salaries and plusher surroundings).

All of these factors intermingle, as may be appreciated by reflecting on the growth of the 'corporate classsroom'. It was recently estimated that fully half of all spending on higher education comes from the corporate sector (*The Economist*, 28 October 1995). IBM, for instance, not only spends over 1 billion dollars per year on research and development, but also boasts eight of its own campuses in which it offers its own university-level education. Of course, most corporations have not gone it alone to such a degree as IBM. Rather they have bought into the established universities, utilizing a series of deals such as sponsored chairs, fellowships, investment in research, customized courses, and close consultancy relationships. The process has noticeably accelerated of late as universities have become more market-sensitive and have made themselves more willing to work with industrial partners, and higher education has accordingly changed its form, abandoning in the eyes of many its traditional priorities and principles.

It might plausibly be suggested that these amount to a breakdown of the established university, or at the least to a decisive shift towards a postmodern higher education. These trends cannot be denied as matters of empirical fact. However, against the interpretation that the university is being overturned, it can be insisted that the virtual monopoly the university retains in the awarding of legitimate credentials testifies to academe's vitality. Admittedly there has been some increased involvement of professional bodies even in this area, with repeated demands that particular course contents are a requisite of professional validation, and there has been a rash of franchising in which some universities have had their reputations tarnished. However, there has been a long history of professional bodies, notably medicine and law, contributing to the internal life of universities and, while the balance may tilt too far one way or another at any given time, checks and balances have been put in place to sustain academic autonomy and tradition. Moreover, the practice of franchising, in spite of the terminology, is no new thing – for instance, the University of London operated for years an external degree programme without it being thought that this might signal the end of the university.

We are back here to emphasizing the adaptability of the university, such that change can be handled in ways which ensure the continuity of defining traditions. In the present period it seems to us a most revealing feature that universities are maintaining the monopoly of bestowing degrees. No doubt it is possible to learn all one's high-level electronic engineering from BT, all one's computer science from IBM, and even one's economics from the Treasury. A handful of companies, chiefly knowledge-intensive organizations such as Arthur D. Little, the management consultancy business, even grant their own master's degrees. These might be expected to grow in the coming years. However, give or take the few exceptions, the fact remains that qualifications from such sources carry much less credibility than those authorized by the universities. This is so in the eyes not only of students and the general public, but frequently also of the corporate sector itself.

It seems to us that the accrediting function remains an important index of a constant and crucial element of higher education, since the widespread acknowledgement of the university's right to bestow qualifications highlights public recognition of essential qualities that constitute a genuine university. Above all, these lie in the recognition that university work cannot be reduced to the merely functional, instrumental and interested. McDonald's reputedly awards degrees at a McBurger University near Chicago, and the Disney organization is rumoured to be interested in expanding from 'infotainment' to producing graduates. But examples such as these are instanced, as a rule, by way of a ridiculous joke, a *reductio ad absurdum* of some trends in higher education. They do not signal a likely outcome of real-world developments because, to the contrary, the very legitimacy of university credentials hinges on public confidence that the teaching and learning that takes place there, and the research which accompanies and frequently undergirds it, are guided by higher ideals than the commercial and instrumental. This is what Paul Filmer (Chapter 5) describes here as the principle of *disinterestedness*. It is a quality which, if not altogether absent in the corporate sector, is always threatened with subordination to the prior concerns of business organizations.

These sorts of argument are, of course, antipathetic to the postmodern temper which – parodying here Marxist shibboleths – insists that absolutely *everything* is about interests, though to the postmodern analyst there is such a multiplicity of interests of gender, identity, age, status, privilege and so on, that no single interest predominates. Yet these ideals seem to us still a critical element of university life which, if put under some strain, remain resonant and indeed defining features of the university. We would add that this quality is more than mere assurance of the university's independence to construct and assess courses as it deems most appropriate. It also entails an insistence that a university education is about a great deal more than transmission of knowledge and techniques which would allow those who have mastered them to perform a given occupation. We refer, of course, to qualities such as the conduct of critical enquiry and rational debate, nurturing abilities such as a capacity to distinguish opinion from evidence and to evaluate an argument dispassionately, to learn independently and in groups, to develop abilities to present coherent arguments, to improve the sophistication of one's thinking, to open one's imagination and reflexive capabilities, to improve analytical capacities, and to think conceptually. Hard to measure these may be, and often academics are reticent to claim they achieve them, but that they are cultivated inside universities as we know them is indisputable (cf. Pascarella and Terenzini, 1991; Astin, 1993).

We cannot guarantee that all university courses and all university students develop all of these qualities, nor even that they will be exposed to them. And we would not want to insist that they cannot be developed elsewhere. We would claim none the less that they are a great deal more difficult to inculcate outside the university than within – Krishan Kumar (Chapter 3) is surely right to stress the importance of the university as a particular sort of gathering place – and we would contend that the university, in so far as it is a place of education, is the primary institution for their pursuit, something evident in its statutes, its value system, and its day-to-day patterns of behaviour.

It appears to us that this is also recognized by the wider society, even by corporate donors to the university. It is right that concern is expressed when corporations come to provide an increasing percentage of the university's resources, for the obvious reason that private companies are not unthinkingly altruistic and have interests of their own to pursue. Few people are unaware that 'industry' tends to give support to departments of management, finance and the applied sciences, turning its back on less 'relevant' disciplines such as anthropology, philosophy and history. There are exceptions to this drift, from which the decorative arts have been important beneficiaries, but the emphasis is plain enough. There is no inherent educational superiority of the former subject areas, but disproportionate support easily can lead to an imbalanced university where goals and priorities are seriously disturbed. It is also worrisome when academics become over-assiduous in wooing corporate sponsors, perhaps becoming supine and promising more than is proper in the process (cf. Thompson, 1970). Yet there is a long tradition of private donation to the university, one from which we might take some comfort, since for the most part donors have acknowledged the essential need for university autonomy, hence acceding to its statutes and strictures on such contributions coming without binding conditions.

## The public interest

Within the university there has a been a great deal of concern expressed as regards the disproportionate part played by the corporate world. Colleagues mutter in common rooms about the expansion of subject areas such as tourism and retail management, the new Tesco chair in business administration, and frequently moan that this is the road to ruin for higher education. Such criticism has readily broadened to concern being voiced about excessive vocationalism in the construction of the curriculum, though in truth it is government rather than industry that has insisted most loudly on higher education being more intimately tied to this 'real world'.

We share much of the apprehension towards such developments. However, what cannot be resisted is the point posed so sharply by Bill Melody in this collection (Chapter 7). Higher education, while it is a distinctly individual experience for the students, is simultaneously deeply embroiled in public policy. This is not just because the lion's share of funding comes from the public purse (though the argument for greater accountability for public money has merit and universities should continue to improve the transparency of their operations). It is also because higher education necessarily involves collective ends such as economic performance, the directions of research, the nation's stocks of knowledge, and even the quality of democratic debate.

A central collective goal is that of equality of opportunity, largely if not only to compete for places in the occupational hierarchy which access to higher education either facilitates or denies. For this reason alone one cannot envisage, still less propose, a return of the university to its pre-expansionary period, since so many were then excluded that such a suggestion has become indefensible. The spread of higher education, hesitantly in the 1960s and then rapidly since the mid-1980s, has opened up opportunities for very many more than have been able to experience university ever before, and this must be a reason for celebration.

However, this has been accompanied by an apparent reinforcement of the hold on places at the most prestigious universities by those from the more privileged backgrounds. Selection of students on the basis of attained scores in public examinations – an obvious and important application of the principle of equal opportunities – has been best adapted to by those most alert towards, and most capable of preparing for, success at A level and GCSE. Thus the best universities, now committed to choosing their students on the basis of demonstrable achievement and irrespective of judgements about family background or character, still find themselves stocked by candidates from a narrow segment of the class structure, especially the children of the professional middle classes who appear remarkably able to achieve A level scores of 28 points and above.

Precisely how to respond to this development is a complex matter which will require varied local responses, yet it remains one of public policy which needs to be addressed by the universities. The principle of equality of opportunity to participate in higher education is now well founded, but the means for achieving this remain flawed. This is certainly not to say that performance in open examinations is to be gainsaid, since this was undoubtedly an advance on the pre-war days of selection of the 'right sort of chap'. However, if we are to aspire to genuine equal opportunities still more needs to be done, and this requires that results at A level be supplemented by other sorts of information and judgement about candidates. Oddly enough, it is precisely the least prestigious universities that have adopted the most flexible criteria of admission, something that reflects both the competition for places and a more generous concept of educability.

## Intellectuals and the university

Any consideration of the public interest and the university must turn, sooner or later, to the position of intellectuals, for the obvious reason that such a large proportion of those whose role it is to reflect on and contribute to the ways in which society sees and constructs itself have found a home inside academe. In this book we have encountered two interpretation of intellectuals today which, from very different directions, come to much the same conclusion. Russell Jacoby (Chapter 6) argues eloquently that the growth of the universities has signalled the end of the public intellectual – one who aspired at least to address a wide public about matters of common concern – because, while providing an economic haven for the intellectual, it has led to writing that improves the prospects of promotion within the university rather than contributing to public affairs. A manifestation of this is the convoluted and self-referential – and socially exclusive – language of so many of today's university intellectuals whose 'radicalism' finds expression in essays on matters such as 'how phallocentricity is inscribed in Dickens' portrayal of Little Nell' at a time when the 'world changes more deeply, widely, thrillingly than at any moment since 1917, perhaps since 1848' (Hughes, 1993, p. 72).

From quite another wing proponents of the postmodern university announce the defrocking of the universal intellectual (who had the arrogance to write under the supposition that they, seeing more keenly, could guide readers to a better world) and the establishment of something much more modest, a *specific* intellectual who offers local, deeply textured and specialized knowledges without any claim to an authoritative position. Here the postmodern intellectual, to adopt Professor Bauman's (1987) terminology, is an interpreter rather than a legislator. The presumptuousness of the universal intellectual has gone, thrown aside by alternative and frequently contesting and contradictory sources of knowledge, displaced by multiple knowledges which may coexist 'playfully', but yet are typically impenetrable for all but the few cognoscenti. The conclusion is a situation much like that described by Jacoby – a university system incapable of and not disposed to engaging with a wider public and public issues.

We can recognize aspects of this in many areas of university life today: in the incessant specialization that can so readily isolate; in recondite vocabularies that can appear barriers to comprehension; perhaps also in a decline in public regard for university academics which may be gauged in the fall in their relative earnings and in caricatures of ineffective and feckless scholars. However, we cannot go so far as either Jacoby or Bauman, either with the pessimism of one who laments the incorporation of intellectuals into the university career structure or with the more positive interpretation of intellectual 'multi-vocalism' in the postmodern world.

There are both empirical and normative reasons for rejecting these two scenarios. Certainly it seems that the retreat of intellectuals can be overstated. Indeed, the very success of think-tanks and broadsheet newspapers outside of academe owes a good deal to regular involvement of university personnel, as also it testifies to the ability of higher education to cultivate able intellectuals who continue in later life to develop and draw upon qualities that have been nurtured in the university. Moreover, when one reflects on the widespread respect for the university, for its ideals and practices, as well as public willingness to acknowledge the legitimacy of university credentials, then this must lead one to be sceptical of postmodern claims that intellectuals have lost credibility.

Similarly, those who describe the postmodern intellectual over-emphasize the fragmentation that has occurred on recent years. There has been, undeniably, a decline in the confidence of intellectuals, but, against this, it is hard to conceive of any major cultural shift in the post-war world that has not closely engaged the university intellectual – and this covers every major intellectual fashion, including postmodernism. There has certainly been a reluctance among intellectuals to offer blueprints for the improvement of society, scarcely surprising in view of the collapse of the boldest blueprint in history – the communist experiment – and recent evidence of the limitations of scientific, and especially technological, progress (Chernobyl, BSE and all the rest). Yet in spite of this there is little evidence to suggest there has been a long-term and radical disengagement of intellectuals from public affairs. On the contrary, one could even argue that there has been something of a resurgence of intellectual involvement in the public domain, for instance by pointing to the extraordinary interest in, and access to, the writings of contemporary scientists such as Stephen Hawking, Richard Dawkins and Stephen Jay Gould.

We neither write off the university as a lost cause with Jacoby, nor conclude, with Bauman, that all is well so long as a multiplicity of different intellectual positions can thrive. We do so because, echoing Jürgen Habermas, we can conceive of the university as a form of *public sphere*, one which, incidentally, has expanded enormously, nationally and internationally, and which operates in key respects as a global village of intellectual exchange. As a public sphere the university has a number of defining characteristics. These include a commitment to rational debate and open argument that is pursued in an impartial, tolerant, open-minded and questioning manner. A prerequisite of the university public sphere is that it maintains a distance from partial interests. This is an especial concern in recent years during which government has been heavy-handed and the corporate world has come to be relied upon by the university considerably more than in the past.

It is something of a paradox that university autonomy must be insisted on as a requisite of supporting an intellectual life that can be actively and effectively involved in public affairs. Yet it is the case that intellectual life must be at one and the same time *apart* from wider interests and *closely engaged* in the wider society through its research, curriculum and many other contributions to public affairs. We do not want to over-dramatize this tension: the relationship between the university and its paymasters is never permanently settled, and it must be of necessity a matter of ongoing negotiation. However, the autonomy of the university must be defended, though it may, especially now, appear to be a self-serving defence, if its role in the public sphere is to continue and thrive. Intellectuals in the university can act, to borrow from Auden, as an 'affirming flame' for the cultural life of a society. To ensure the flame burns brightly, the wider society needs must keep its distance while supplying the fuel.

# Note

1. Gibbons *et al.* (1994, p. 3) distinguish knowledges as follows : 'in Mode 1 problems are set and solved in a context governed by the, largely academic, interests of a specific community. By contrast, Mode 2 knowledge is carried out in a context of application. Mode 1 is disciplinary while Mode 2 is transdisciplinary. Mode 1 is characterised by homogeneity, Mode 2 by heterogeneity. Organisationally, Mode 1 is hierarchical and tends to preserve its form, while Mode 2 is more heterarchical and transient. Each employs a different type of quality control. In comparison with Mode 1, Mode 2 is more socially accountable and reflexive'.

# References

Ahmad, A. (1992) *In Theory: Classes, Nations, Literatures.* London: Verso.

Amin, A. (ed.) (1994) *Post-Fordism: A Reader.* Oxford: Blackwell.

Anderson, C.W. (1993) *Prescribing the Life of the Mind: An Essay on the Purpose of the University, the Aims of Liberal Education, the Competence of Citizens, and the Cultivation of Practical Reason.* Madison: University of Wisconsin Press.

Anderson, M. (1992) *Imposters in the Temple.* New York: Simon and Schuster.

Anderson, P. (1968) 'Components of the National Culture', *New Left Review*, 50, May–June. Reprinted in Alexander Cockburn and Robin Blackburn (eds) (1969) *Student Power: Problems, Diagnosis, Action.* Harmondsworth: Penguin, pp. 214–84.

Arnold, M. (1983) *Culture and Anarchy.* New York: Chelsea House. First published in 1867.

Ashton, D. (1986) *Unemployment under Capitalism.* Brighton: Wheatsheaf.

Association of Graduate Recruiters (AGR) (1996) *Skills for Graduates in the 21st Century.* Cambridge: AGR.

Astin, A.W. (1993) *What Matters in College: Four Critical Years Revisited.* San Francisco: Jossey-Bass.

Ball, C. (1990) 'More Means Different: Wider Participation in Better Higher Education', *Journal of the Royal Society of Arts* (RSA), October, 743–57.

Barnett, R. (1990) *The Idea of Higher Education.* Buckingham: Society for Research into Higher Education/Open University Press.

Barnett, R. (1994) *The Limits of Competence: Knowledge, Higher Education and Society.* Buckingham: Society for Research into Higher Education/Open University Press.

Barrès, M. (1925) *Scènes et Doctrines du Nationalisme*, Vol. 1. Paris: Librarie Plon.

Bauman, Z. (1987) *Legislators and Interpreters: On Modernity, Postmodernity, and the Intellectual.* Cambridge: Polity.

Beck, U. (1992) *Risk Society: Towards a New Modernity.* London: Sage.

Bell, D. (1966) *The Reforming of General Education: The Columbia College Experience in its National Setting.* New York: Columbia University Press.

Bell, D. (1976) *The Coming of Post-Industrial Society: A Venture in Social Forecasting.* Harmondsworth: Penguin. First published in 1973.

Bering, D. (1978) *Die Intellektuellen: Geschichte eines Schimpfwortes.* Stuttgart: Ernst Klett Verlag.

Bernstein, B. (1975) *Class, Codes and Control: Vol. 3, Towards a Theory of Educational Transmissions.* London: Routledge & Kegan Paul.

Blair, T. (1996) *New Britain: My Vision of a Young Country* (ed. Ian Hargreaves). London: Fourth Estate.

Bloom, A. (1987) *The Closing of the American Mind: How Higher Education Has Failed Democracy and Impoverished the Souls of Today's Students.* New York: Simon & Schuster.

Bok, D. (1982) *Beyond the Ivory Tower: Social Responsibilities of the Modern University.* Cambridge, MA: Harvard University Press.

Bonney, N. (1996) 'The Careers of University Graduates: The Classes of 1960 and 1985'. Paper presented to the conference on 'Dilemmas of Mass Higher Education', Staffordshire University, 10–12 April.

Bourdieu, P. and Passeron, J.-C. (1964) *The Inheritors: French Students and Their Relation to Culture.* Chicago: University of Chicago Press.

Bowles, S. and Gintis, H. (1976) *Schooling in Capitalist America.* London: Routledge.

Boyer, E.L. (1987) *College: The Undergraduate Experience in America.* The Carnegie Foundation for the Advancement of Teaching. New York: Harper & Row.

Brown, P. (1995) 'Cultural Capital and Social Exclusion: Some Observations on Recent Trends in Education, Employment and the Labour Market', *Work, Employment and Society*, 9, 29–51.

Brown, P. and Lauder, H. (1992) 'Education, Economy and Society: An Introduction to a New Agenda'. In P. Brown and H. Lauder (eds) *Education for Economic Survival: From Fordism to Post-Fordism.* London: Routledge.

Brown, P. and Scase, R. (1994) *Higher Education and Corporate Realities: Class, Culture and the Decline of Graduate Careers.* London: UCL Press.

Buchbinder, H. (1993) 'The Market Oriented University and the Changing Role of Knowledge', *Higher Education*, 26, 331–47.

Callender, C. and Kempson, E. (1996) *Student Finances: A Survey of Student Income and Expenditure.* London: Policy Studies Institute.

Carnevale, A. and Porro, J. (1994) *Quality Education: School Reform for the New American Economy.* Washington, DC: US Department of Education.

Carswell, J. (1985) *Government and Universities in Britain – 1960–80.* Cambridge: Cambridge University Press.

Carter, I. (1990) *Ancient Cultures of Conceit: British University Fiction in the Post-War Years.* London: Routledge.

Caul, B. (1993) *Value-Added: The Personal Development of Students in Higher Education.* Belfast: December Publications.

Clark, B. (1983) *The Higher Education System: Academic Organisation in Cross-National Perspective.* Berkeley: University of California Press.

Cockett, R. (1994) *Thinking the Unthinkable.* London: HarperCollins.

Cohen, P. (1995) 'Thinking Globally, Acting Locally'. In *For a Multicultural University*, Working Paper 3, December. London: The New Ethnicities Unit, University of East London.

Committee on Higher Education (1963) *Higher Education*, Cmnd. 2154 (Robbins Report). London: HMSO.

Confederation of British Industry (CBI) (1994) *Thinking Ahead: Ensuring the Expansion of Higher Education into the 21st Century.* London: CBI.

Crompton, R. and Sanderson, K. (1990) *Gendered Jobs and Social Change.* London: Unwin Hyman.

Culler, J. (1988) *Framing the Sign: Criticism and its Institutions.* Norman: University of Oaklahoma Press.

Curtius, E.R. (1990) 'Sociology and its Limits'. In V. Meja and N. Stehr (eds), *Knowledge and Politics: The Sociology of Knowledge Dispute.* New York: Routledge.

Davie, G. (1961) *The Democratic Intellect.* Edinburgh: Edinburgh University Press.
Davie, G. (1986) *The Crisis of the Democratic Intellect.* Edinburgh: Polygon.
Davies, I. (1993) 'Cultural Theory in Britain: Narrative and Episteme', *Theory, Culture and Society,* 10(3).
Debray, R. (1979) *Le Pouvoir Intellectuel en France.* Paris: Ramsay.
Derrida, J. (1986) *Margins of Philosophy* (trans. Alan Bass). Chicago: University of Chicago Press.
Dominelli, L. and Hoogvelt, A. (1996) 'Globalisation, Contract Government and the Taylorisation of Intellectual Labour in Academia', *Studies in Political Economy,* 49 (Spring).
Drozdowicz, Z. (1995) *Excellentia Universitas.* Poznań: Humaniora.
Eagleton, T. (1994) 'Discourse and Discos', *The Times Literary Supplement,* 15 June.
Eley, G. (1992) 'Nations, Public, and Political Cultures'. In C. Calhoun (ed.), *Habermas and the Public Sphere.* Cambridge, MA: MIT Press.
Eliot, T.S. (1948) *Notes Towards the Definition of Culture.* London: Faber and Faber.
Eyerman, R. (1994) *Between Culture and Politics: Intellectuals in Modern Society.* Cambridge: Polity Press.
Featherstone, M., Lash, S. and Robertson, R. (1995) *Global Modernities.* London: Sage.
Fraser, N. (1992), 'Rethinking the Public Sphere'. In C. Calhoun (ed.) *Habermas and the Public Sphere.* Cambridge, MA: MIT Press.
Freeman, C. and Perez, C. (1988) 'Structural Crises of Adjustment, Business Cycles and Investment Behaviour'. In G. Dosi, C. Freeman, R. Nelson, G. Silverberg and L. Soete (eds) *Technical Change and Economic Theory.* London: Pinter.
Fromm, E. (1962), 'Personality and the Market Place'. In S. Nosow and W. Form (eds), *Man, Work and Society.* New York: Basic Books.
Gerth, H. and Mills, C.W. (1958) *From Max Weber: Essays in Sociology.* New York: Oxford University Press.
Gibbons, M., Limoges, C., Nowotny, H., Schwartzman, S., Scott, P. and Trow, M. (1994), *The New Production of Knowledge: The Dynamics of Science and Research in Contemporary Societies.* London: Sage.
Gibbs, G. (ed.) (1996) *Using Research to Improve Student Learning.* Oxford: Oxford Centre for Staff Development.
Gibbs, G., Lucas, L. and Webster, F. (forthcoming) 'Class Size, Assessment and Student Performance in Sociology in a British University: 1984–94', *Teaching Sociology.*
Goffee, R. and Scase, R. (1989) *Reluctant Managers: Their Work and Life Styles.* London: Routledge.
Gorz, A. (1982) *Farewell to the Working Class: An Essay on Post-Industrial Socialism* (translated by Michael Sonenscher). Pluto Press. First published in 1980.
Gorz, A. (1985) *Paths to Paradise: On the Liberation from Work,* translated by Malcolm Imrie. Pluto Press. First published in 1983.
Gramsci, A. (1971) *Selections from the Prison Notebooks* (ed. and trans. Q. Hoare and G.N. Smith). London: Lawrence and Wishart.
Hague, Sir Douglas (1991) *Beyond Universities: A New Republic of the Intellect.* London: Institute of Economic Affairs.
Hague, Sir Douglas (1996) 'Knowledge Goes Out to Market', *Times Higher Education Supplement,* 24 May, p. 12.
Hall, S. (1980) 'Cultural Studies and the Centre: Some Problematics and Problems'. In Stuart Hall, D. Hobson, A. Lowe and P. Willis (eds), *Culture, Media, Language: Working Papers in Cultural Studies.* London: Hutchinson, pp. 15–47.

Halsey, A.H. (1992) *Decline of Donnish Dominion: The British Academic Professions in the Twentieth Century*. Oxford: Clarendon Press.

Handy, C. (1989) *The Age of Unreason*. London: Hutchinson.

Hebdige, D. (1988) *Hiding in the Light: On Images and Things*. London: Comedia.

Higher Education Quality Council (HEQC) (1996a) *Inter-Institutional Variability of Degree Results: An Analysis in Selected Areas*. London: HEQC.

Higher Education Quality Council (HEQC) (1996b) *Academic Standards in the Approval, Review and Classification of Degrees*. London: HEQC.

Hirsch, E.D. (1987) *Cultural Literacy: What Every American Should Know*. Boston: Houghton Mifflin.

Hirsch, F. (1977) *The Social Limits to Growth*. London: Routledge & Kegan Paul.

Hoeges, D. (1994) *Kontroverse am Abgrund: Ernst Robert Curtius und Karl Mannheim*. Frankfurt: Fischer.

hooks, b. (1995) *Killing Rage: Ending Racism*. New York: Henry Holt.

Hughes, R. (1993) *Culture of Complaint: The Fraying of America*. New York: Oxford University Press.

Innis, H. (1951) *The Bias of Communication*. Toronto: University of Toronto Press.

Jacoby, H. (1973) *The Bureaucratization of the World*. Berkeley: California University Press.

Jenkins, R. (1985) 'Black Workers in the Labour Market: The Price of Recession'. In B. Roberts, R. Finnigan and D. Gallie (eds), *New Approaches to Economic Life*. Manchester: Manchester University Press.

Judt, T. (1992) *Past Imperfect: French Intellectuals, 1944–1956*. Berkeley: University of California Press.

Kanter, R. (1989) *When Giants Learn to Dance*. New York: Simon and Schuster.

Kerr, C. (1963) *The Uses of the University*. Cambridge, MA: Harvard University Press.

Kumar, K. (1997) 'Home: The Promise and Predicament of Private Life at the End of the Twentieth Century'. In Jeff Weintraub and Krishan Kumar (eds), *Private and Public in Thought and Practice*. Chicago: University of Chicago Press.

Laurillard, D. (1993) *Rethinking University Teaching*. London: Routledge.

Leavis, F.R. (1948) *Education and the University: A Sketch for an 'English School'* (new and enlarged edition). London: Chatto and Windus.

Leavis, F.R. (1969) *English Literature in Our Time and the University*. London: Chatto and Windus.

Lucas, L. and Webster, F. (1997) 'Maintaining Standards: A Case Study'. In D. Jary and M. Parker (eds), *Dilemmas of Mass Higher Education*. Staffordshire University Press. Shortened version published in Webster (1996).

Lyotard, J.-F. (1984a) *The Postmodern Condition*. Manchester: Manchester University Press.

Lyotard, J.-F. (1984b) *Tombeau de l'Intellectuel et Autres Papiers*. Paris: Editions Galilée.

Lyotard, J.-F. (1993) *Political Writings* (trans. Bill Readings and Kevin Paul Geiman). London: UCL Press.

Mannheim, K. (1940) *Man and Society: In the Age of Reconstruction*. London: Kegan Paul.

Mannheim, K. (1985) *Ideology and Utopia* (trans. L. Wirth and E. Shils). San Diego, CA: Harcourt Brace Jovanovich.

Marquand, O. (1987) *Apologie des Zufälligen*. Stuttgart: Phillip Reclam.

McLeish, J. (1991) *Number*. New York: Fawcett Columbine.

Melody, W.H. (1990a) 'Communication Policy in the Global Information Economy: Whither the Public Interest?'. In Marjorie Ferguson (ed.), *Public Communication: The New Imperatives*. London: Sage.

Melody, W.H. (1990b) 'The Information in IT: Where Lies the Public Interest?', *Intermedia*, 18(3).

Merton, R. (1967) *Social Theory and Social Structure*. New York: Free Press.

Meyerson, M. (1975) 'After a Decade of the Levelers in Higher Education: Reinforcing Quality While Maintaining Mass Education', *Daedalus: Journal of the American Academy of Arts and Sciences*, 104(1).

Minogue, K.R. (1973) *The Concept of a University*. London: Weidenfeld & Nicolson.

Moberly, Sir Walter (1949) *The Crisis in the University*. London: SCM Press.

Mulhern, F. (1979) *The Moment of Scrutiny*. London: New Left Books.

Newman, J.H. (1987) *The Idea of a University, Defined and Illustrated* (ed. Daniel M. O'Connell). Chicago: Loyola University Press. First published in 1853.

Nisbet, R.A. (1996) *The Degradation of the Academic Dogma* (2nd edition). New York: Transaction Publishers. First published in 1972.

Nowotny, H. (1994) *Time: The Modern and Postmodern Experience*. Cambridge: Polity Press.

Office of Science and Technology (1995) *Technology Foresight 14: Leisure and Learning*. London: HMSO.

Ontario Council on University Affairs (1994) *Undergraduate Teaching, Research and Consulting/Community Service: What are the Functional Interactions? A Literature Survey*. Toronto: Task Force on Resource Allocation.

Parsons, T. and Platt, G.M. (1973) *The American University*. Cambridge, MA: Harvard University Press.

Pascarella, E. and Terenzini, P.T. (1991) *How College Affects Students: Findings and Insights from Twenty Years of Research*. San Francisco: Jossey-Bass.

Peters, T.J. and Waterman, R.H. (1982) *In Search of Excellence*. New York: Harper & Row.

Phillips, M. (1996) *All Must Have Prizes*. London: Little Brown.

Purcell, K. and Pitcher, J. (1996) *Great Expectations: The New Diversity of Graduate Skills and Aspirations*. Manchester: Careers Services Unit.

Rabinbach, A. (1983) *The Crisis of Austrian Socialism: From Red Vienna to Civil War, 1927–1934*. Chicago: University of Chicago Press.

Readings, B. (1996) *The University in Ruins*. Cambridge, MA: Harvard University Press.

Reich, W. (1976) *People in Trouble*, Vol. 2 (trans. P. Schmitz). New York: Farrar, Straus and Giroux.

Ribeiro, A. (1995) 'Von einem Fin de Siècle zum nächsten', *Mittelweg* (Zeitschrift des Hamburger Instituts für Sozialforschung), 36, 10–12.

Ritzer, G. (1996) 'Fighting Fire with Fire: (Mostly) Rational Responses to the Rationalization Crisis in Higher Education'. Paper presented to the conference on 'Dilemmas of Mass Higher Education', Staffordshire University, 10–12 April.

Robbins, B. (ed.) (1993) *The Phantom Public Sphere*. Minneapolis: University of Minnesota Press.

Rose, N. (1989) *Governing the Soul: The Shaping of the Private Self*. London: Routledge.

Ross, A. (1989) *No Respect: Intellectuals and Popular Culture*. New York: Routledge.

Rothblatt, S. (1996) 'Road to Lonely Learning', *Times Higher Education Supplement*, 2 August, p. 14.

Ryan, A. (1996) 'Propagate a New Ivy Variety', *Times Higher Education Supplement*, 29 November, p. 12.

Said, E. (1994) *Representations of the Intellectual*. London: Vintage.

Sanderson, M. (1972) *The Universities and British Industry, 1850–1970*. London: Routledge & Kegan Paul.

Scase, R. (1992) *Class: An Introduction*. Buckingham: Open University Press.

Scase, R. and Goffee, R. (1995) *Corporate Realities: The Dynamics of Large and Small Organisations*. London: Routledge.

Scott, P. (1984) *The Crisis of the University*. London: Croom Helm.

Scott, P. (1995) *The Meanings of Mass Higher Education*. Buckingham: Society for Research into Higher Education/Open University Press.

Shils, E. (1965) 'Charisma, Order and Status', *American Sociological Review*, 30, 199–213.

Smith, A. (1989) 'The Public Interest', *Intermedia*, 17(2), 10–24. Reprinted in Anthony Smith (1993) *Books to Bytes: Knowledge and Information in the Postmodern Era*. London: British Film Institute, Chapter 4.

Smith, D., Scott, P. and Lynch, J. (1995) *The Role of Marketing in the University and College Sector*. Leeds: Higher Education Information Services Trust (HEIST) Publications.

Smith, V. (1989) *Managing in the Corporate Interest*. Berkeley: University of California Press.

Sokal, A.D. (1996a) 'Transgressing the Boundaries: Toward a Transformative Hermeneutics of Quantum Gravity', *Social Text*, 46–7.

Sokal, A.D. (1996b) 'A Physicist Experiments with Cultural Studies', *Lingua Franca*, May–June, 62–4.

Sokal, A.D. (1996c) 'Postmodern Gravity Deconstructed, Slyly', *New York Times*, 18 May, p. A-1.

Speier, H. (1990) 'Sociology or Ideology?' [1930]. In V. Meja and N. Stehr (eds), *Knowledge and Politics: The Sociology of Knowledge Dispute*. New York: Routledge.

Spivak, G.C. (1993) *Outside in the Teaching Machine*. New York: Routledge.

Sykes, C.J. (1988) *Profscam: Professors and the Demise of Higher Education*. Washington, DC: Regnery Gateway.

Thompson, E.P. (1970) 'The Business University'. In E.P. Thompson, *Writing by Candlelight*. London: Merlin, pp. 13–27.

Trow, M. (1970) 'Reflections on the Transition from Elite to Mass Higher Education', *Daedalus: Journal of the American Academy of Arts and Sciences*, 90(1), 1–42.

Trow, M. (1973) *Problems in the Transition from Elite to Mass Higher Education*. Berkeley, CA: Carnegie Commission on Higher Education.

Vogt, J. (1993) 'Have the Intellectuals Failed? On the Sociological Claims and the Influence of Literary Intellectuals in West Germany', *New German Critique*, 58, 3–24.

Voltaire (1972) 'Lettres'. In *Philosophical Dictionary* (ed. T. Besterman). New York: Penguin.

Wagner, L. (1995) 'Change and Continuity in Higher Education'. Inaugural lecture, Leeds Metropolitan University.

Walden, G. (1996) *We Should Know Better: Solving the Education Crisis*. London: Fourth Estate.

Wall, I.M. (1994) 'From Anti-Americanism to Francophobia: The Saga of French and American Intellectuals', *French Historical Studies*, 18, 1083–1100.

Wallas, G. (1934) *Social Judgment*. London: George Allen & Unwin.

Walzer, M. (1987) *Interpretation and Social Criticism*. Cambridge, MA: Harvard University Press.

Walzer, M. (1988) *The Company of Critics: Social Criticism and Political Commitment in the Twentieth Century*. New York: Basic Books.

Warner, M. (1993) 'The Mass Public and the Mass Subject'. In Bruce Robbins (ed.), *The Phantom Public Sphere*. Minneapolis: University of Minnesota Press.

Waterman, R., Waterman, J. and Collard, B. (1994) 'Toward a Career-Resilient Workforce', *Harvard Business Review*, 72(4), 87–95.

Watson, D. (1996) *The Limits of Diversity*. Keynote paper presented to the conference on the 'The Dilemmas of Mass Higher Education', Staffordshire University, 10–12 April.

Watts, A.G. (1996) *Careerquake*. London: Demos.

Weber, M. (1948) *From Max Weber: Essays in Sociology*. (ed. and trans. H.H. Gerth and C. Wright Mills). London: Routledge & Kegan Paul.

Webster, F. (1996) 'Art of Course Assessment', *The Times Higher Education Supplement*, 24 May, p. 13.

Whitehead, A.N. (1964) *Science and the Modern World*. New York: Mentor Books.

Whyte, W.H. (1965) *The Organization Man*. Harmondsworth: Penguin.

Wiener, M. (1981) *English Culture and the Decline of the Industrial Spirit, 1850–1980*. Cambridge: Cambridge University Press.

Wilensky, H. (1960) 'Work, Careers, and Social Integration', *International Social Science Journal*, 12, 543–60.

Wittfogel, K. (1990) 'Knowledge and Society' [1931]. In V. Meja and N. Stehr (eds), *Knowledge and Politics: The Sociology of Knowledge Dispute*. New York: Routledge.

# Index

# The Society for Research into Higher Education

The Society for Research into Higher Education exists to stimulate and coordinate research into all aspects of higher education. It aims to improve the quality of higher education through the encouragement of debate and publication on issues of policy, on the organization and management of higher education institutions, and on the curriculum and teaching methods.

The Society's income is derived from subscriptions, sales of its books and journals, conference fees and grants. It receives no subsidies, and is wholly independent. Its individual members include teachers, researchers, managers and students. Its corporate members are institutions of higher education, research institutes, professional, industrial and governmental bodies. Members are not only from the UK, but from elsewhere in Europe, from America, Canada and Australasia, and it regards its international work as among its most important activities.

Under the imprint *SRHE & Open University Press*, the Society is a specialist publisher of research, having some 60 titles in print. The Editorial Board of the Society's Imprint seeks authoritative research or study in the above fields. It offers competitive royalties, a highly recognizable format in both hardback and paperback and the worldwide reputation of the Open University Press.

The Society also publishes *Studies in Higher Education* (three times a year), which is mainly concerned with academic issues, *Higher Education Quarterly* (formerly *Universities Quarterly*), mainly concerned with policy issues, *Research into Higher Education Abstracts* (three times a year), and *SRHE News* (four times a year).

The Society holds a major annual conference in December, jointly with an institution of higher education. In 1994 the topic was 'The Student Experience' at the University of York. In 1995 it was 'The Changing University' at Heriot-Watt University in Edinburgh and in 1996, 'Working in Higher Education' at Cardiff Institute of Higher Education. Conferences in 1997 include 'Beyond the First Degree' at the University of Warwick.

The Society's committees, study groups and branches are run by the members. The groups at present include:

Teacher Education Study Group
Continuing Education Group
Staff Development Group
Excellence in Teaching and Learning

# Benefits to members

## *Individual*

Individual members receive:

- *SRHE News*, the Society's publications list, conference details and other material included in mailings.
- Greatly reduced rates for *Studies in Higher Education* and *Higher Education Quarterly*.
- A 35 per cent discount on all SRHE & Open University Press publications.
- Free copies of the Proceedings – commissioned papers on the theme of the Annual Conference.
- Free copies of *Research into Higher Education Abstracts*.
- Reduced rates for conferences.
- Extensive contacts and scope for facilitating initiatives.
- Reduced reciprocal memberships.
- Free copies of the *Register of Members' Research Interests*.

## *Corporate*

Corporate members receive:

- All benefits of individual members, plus.
- Free copies of *Studies in Higher Education*.
- Unlimited copies of the Society's publications at reduced rates.
- Special rates for its members e.g. to the Annual Conference.
- The right to submit application for the Society's  research grants.

 *Membership details*: SRHE, 3 Devonshire Street, London WIN 2BA, UK. Tel: 0171 637 2766. Fax: 0171 637 2781. email: srhe@mailbox1.ulcc.ac.uk
World Wide Web: http://www.srhe.ac.uk./srhe
*Catalogue*: SRHE & Open University Press, Celtic Court, 22 Ballmoor, Buckingham MK18 1XW. Tel: 01280 823388. Fax: 01280 823233. email: enquiries@openup.co.uk